Appalachian Trail
Thru-Hike Planner

Protect, enhance, and promote

the Trail experience:

That's what we do

You can help

by joining the

Appalachian Trail Conservancy today!

You can become a member by going to

www.appalachiantrail.org/join

or calling (304) 535-6331

On the trail, your ATC membership card shows your support for the trail and affords you discounts at some hostels and outfitters—and, before you go or in Harpers Ferry, nets you a discount from the Ultimate A.T. Store®.

Let Us Hear from You

Home to the Appalachian Trail Conservancy, Harpers Ferry, West Virginia, doubles as the psychological midpoint of the Appalachian Trail. Hundreds of thru-hikers and section-hikers stride through the door of our humble headquarters at 799 Washington Street to shoot the breeze and have their photos taken for that year's hiker album. If you're a member, we'll give you a postcard version of your official photo. We hope to see *you* here soon!

In the meantime, drop us a postcard or e-mail from the trail:

Appalachian Trail Conservancy
P.O. Box 807
Harpers Ferry, WV 25425-0807
<www.appalachiantrail.org>
<info@appalachiantrail.org>>

Appalachian Trail
Thru-Hike Planner

APPALACHIAN TRAIL
CONSERVANCY®

Harpers Ferry

Photography credits: Cover, Avery Peak, Maine © Christina Schubert; page 9, Isaac Wiegmann; page 11, 13, Robert and Dorlyn Williams; page 14, Beverly LaFollette; page 17, ATC; page 19, Andrew J. Fay; page 23, Isaac Wiegmann; page 25, John Fletcher; page 26, Frank Logue; page 29, David Miller; page 30, Kathleen Mallow-Sager; page 32, Laurie Potteiger; page 34, David Miller; page 37, Kathleen Mallow-Sager; page 39, Michael Warren; page 40, ATC; page 42, Timothy Cummings; page 43, Alexandra Daley-Clark; page 45, Isaac Wiegmann; page 47, National Oceanic and Atmospheric Administration; page 49, Charles Wilson; page 50, Arthur Gaudet; back cover, Brian Wing.

ISBN 978-1-889386-92-8

Sixth edition. Printed in the United States of America

Editor (2005): David Lauterborn. Significant revisions for all subsequent editions have been supplied by Laurie H. Potteiger, a thru-hiker, section-hiker, and ATC information-services manager.

Foreword

The Appalachian National Scenic Trail is one of the best-known units of America's national park system and the only major one managed for the most part by volunteers under the umbrella of the Appalachian Trail (ATC). While millions of visitors hit the trail each year, only a fraction attempt what you're considering—thru-hiking "the A.T." in one fell swoop.

While no single book can ensure success in such an undertaking, the *Appalachian Trail Thru-Hike Planner* will improve your chances by helping you thoroughly plan your excursion. This edition revises and expands on material assembled by volunteer and thru-hiker Christopher Whalen, first published by ATC in 1992 as the *Appalachian Trail Workbook for Planning Thru-hikes,* and updates mileages to 2015.

Despite the latest backpacking fashions, certain aspects of thru-hiking the A.T. remain unchanged. Consider these quotes from successful (and not-so) thru-hikers:

> *I had the most amazing experiences hiking the A.T. It was exciting, tiring, magical, lonely, frustrating, beautiful, wet, sublime, scary, cold, amazing, boring, hot, humid, surreal, and perfect. It was everything all at once. It was everything I hoped it would be. It was nothing like I expected it would be.* —Megan "Glacier" Supple

> *Trying to hike the Appalachian Trail was the hardest thing I have ever done. I have never been so cold, wet, sore, and generally wretched. It was also the best thing I have ever done.* —Bill Bryson, author, *A Walk in the Woods*

> *The A.T. community is a microcosm of the way people* should *treat each other in the real world.* —Jason "Shepherd" Constantine

> *Finishing the A.T. was like winning the Super Bowl on my way to the electric chair.* —David "Stewball" Ackley

> *The berries, the leaves, the toads, the seasons as they unfolded .... I loved the large and small ways our natural world can bring wonder to our lives.* —Wendy "Uncle Wendy" Miner-Ashby

> *This is a hundred times harder than I ever imagined and a thousand times more rewarding.* —John "Madhatter" Passman

Enjoy this planner—and your hike!

—Appalachian Trail Conservancy

Maine

Contents

How to Use this Workbook

Chapter ☑ Worksheet

At the beginning of each chapter, you'll find a handy little "Chapter Worksheet" box and icon that will direct your attention to a worksheet or chart in the back of the book. The worksheets/charts relate to the topic covered by each chapter and are perforated for easy removal—yes, we want you to tear them out! Each worksheet builds on the next. By the time you're finished, you'll hold in your hands a rough thru-hike itinerary, gear and food checklists, a sample mail-drop schedule, and thorough information about the trail.

Chapter ✓ Worksheet

**Are you ready to rip out your first worksheets?
Find the back-to-back Test Your Trail Savvy
and Trail Terms on pages 61 and 62.
The test is just a fun warm-up exercise —you won't be graded—
while the trail terms will have you talking
like a 2,000-miler in no time!**

So, you've heard about the Appalachian Trail, the public footpath that extends more than 2,189 miles between Maine and Georgia. Maybe you've already spent an afternoon hiking in the woods or ventured up to its high ridges for a weekend of backpacking and camping. Now, crazy as it sounds, something about the trail has captured your imagination, and you're thinking about hiking it from end to end.

Maybe you haven't told anyone yet, but you're starting to make plans. Or, perhaps you've announced to the world you're going to hike the A.T., and now you need to figure out how. Well, you've come to the right place.

First, welcome to the often strange, obsessive, idealistic, and painful, yet wonderful world of long-distance hiking on the trail. You're in for quite an experience.

Hikers today use high-tech equipment and clothing unheard of in 1948, when Earl Shaffer became the first person to report an A.T. thru-hike. But, a person starting out from Springer Mountain in northern Georgia or Katahdin in central Maine still has to traverse more than 2,189 rugged, mountainous miles. It is not now, nor will it ever be, an easy endeavor.

Contrary to popular myth, however, being young and athletic isn't a requirement to thru-hike the A.T. Successful thru-hikers have included schoolkids and septuagenarians, blind men, and a man on crutches. What is critical is the drive and commitment to see it through.

Of course, a rugged six-month thru-hike across 14 states isn't like a weekend RV trip to the lake or a backyard-tent expedition. It's a complicated logistical undertaking that requires you to factor in such variables as time, money, gear, and food, not to mention your fitness and motivation. Even with the best of planning, the odds are stacked against you. Without preparation, though, your chances of finishing are slim.

In the chapters that follow, you'll find the bedrock of current trail wisdom regarding itineraries, weather, budgeting, gear selection, food planning, resupply, health, and hiking safety. Tear-out worksheets and charts at the back will help you draw up initial plans and compile helpful lists to carry with you on the trail. An appendix lists additional resources, including recommended books and helpful Web sites.

We don't claim to have all the answers, and we encourage you to expand the planning process beyond this book. But, be sure to stuff a few bedraggled worksheets in your pack, if only to remind yourself just how far you have traveled from these first tentative scribbles.

HOW TO PRESERVE THE TRAIL

Practice LNT Every Day –
Be the Role Model You Can Be,
In Every Way!

On page 94, you will find the principles of Leave No Trace (LNT), a program of which ATC is an ardent supporter and teacher. But, it all depends on you, the thru-hiker. It's really just thoughtfulness and common courtesy—to Mother Nature and to the thousands of volunteers who put in their time, year after year, to make the A.T. the special place it is. Because hiking the Trail is a social experience, too, your behavior greatly influences your peers as well as those who wander the woods for a short time without your experience.

Each person seeking to thru-hike the Appalachian Trail does so for different reasons—for fun or exercise, self-discovery or a change of pace, or perhaps to explore nature, walk off grief or misfortune, make new friends, or challenge oneself. A thru-hike offers the time and space to accomplish many such goals.

Approach the trail on its own terms—you'll enjoy it more.

Before you delve into itineraries, worksheets, checklists, and other planning details, consider why you've chosen to thru-hike in the first place. Your reasons will affect the way you plan your hike and your chances of finishing the trail. Ask yourself, *Why do I want to thru-hike?* and whether that reason will sustain you on the trail for six months.

Following are common reasons and strategies toward accomplishing each goal:

I want an adventure—Keep an open schedule, seek the unexpected, and be open to meeting people you otherwise might not encounter in the "real world."

I want to experience nature—Set a leisurely pace, instead of racing along with your head down to finish in time. Leave room in your pack for a camera, journal, and perhaps a field guide or two.

I want solitude and wilderness—Skip the spring exodus at Springer Mountain in favor of a less popular starting time and place. On the trail, stay in a tent, and find your own campsites, rather than staying at shelters, where most hikers congregate.

Motivation

I want to simplify my life—By its nature, a thru-hike is a simple round of eating, sleeping, and walking. Let that rhythm determine your pace. Making plans and meeting people along the way will keep you bound to clocks and calendars.

I want to lose weight—You *will* shed pounds on a thru-hike (see Food, page 39). The trick is to revert to "human" portions and keep the weight off following your hike. Map out a disciplined diet and exercise plan for your return.

I want to get in shape—Start slowly in the first month, hiking just a few miles a day, until your body gets used to the new demands. After that, set your own pace, and enjoy your renewed lung and leg power.

I want to push myself physically—Lighten your load and pare your gear to the bare minimum required for a safe hike. The lighter your pack, the faster and farther you'll walk each day.

I want to make friends, meet kindred spirits—Have fun, but be flexible. If your fellow hikers take a breather in town, you will, too—which may cost a few dollars more. Sharing hardships, scenic beauty, and the desire to finish will draw you closer together.

Choosing a Trail Name

A part of thru-hiking culture is being named by other hikers. However, you may want to have a back-up, in case you don't pick up a trail name or really hate the one conferred on you. To avoid being confused with other hikers, steer clear of such common handles as Bigfoot or Mama Bear. Your trail name should reflect something unique and fitting about your personality—perhaps a character trait, physical attribute, or hobby. Choose carefully, though. Dozens of fellow hikers will refer to you by this handle for several months (or years later at hiker gatherings)—do you really want to be known as Pookie McSnoo or Cheese Foot?

I want to thru-hike with my partner—Share logistical arrangements and be willing to tweak plans to accommodate one another. The weaker partner always sets the pace.

I want to thru-hike with my dog—Plan some prehike training together (both for endurance and obedience). Note that having a dog may encroach on human friendships. Teach your pooch to behave around fellow hikers and refrain from harassing wildlife. Also, some jurisdictions do not allow dogs (you will need to plan for kennels or walk-arounds), and leashes are required on National Park Service lands (about 40 percent of the trail).

Chapter ☑ Worksheet

As you consider a start date, desired pace, and direction, sharpen your pencil, tear out the following worksheets, and sketch out an itinerary. At the back of this book are eight blank Monthly Calendars (page 63) and a Shelters & Towns chart (page 71). The chart lists all shelters, huts, many campsites, and towns along or near the A.T. Where you see long stretches without any listings, consult the *Appalachian Trail Thru-Hikers' Companion*. (See pages 56–57 for more information.) Think in terms of segments, not daily goals. The Sample 180-Day South-North Thru-Hiking Schedule on page 15 will get you started. Have those worksheets handy when you reach the Resupply chapter.

Let's do the math…. The A.T. is more than 2,189 miles long, not counting approach trails. If you average a "leisurely" 10 miles per day, it will take you more than seven months to finish; if you average a brisk 15 miles per day, it will take you slightly less than five months. Most hikers end up somewhere in the middle, averaging 12 miles per day and finishing in about 180 days.

Can you spare six months? For many people, time is the single greatest limiting factor in planning a thru-hike. Six months is a long time to drop out of a career track, go without a paycheck, be away from friends and family, or leave a home vacant. Consequently, most thru-hikers are at transitional times in their lives—just out of college, between jobs or marriages, or retired.

Next is the question of pace. Some extraordinarily fit young hikers try to complete the trail over the course of a summer. A few succeed, but to thru-hike in, say, 110 days means averaging 20 miles a day—a punishing pace that leaves precious little time for anything other than marching from dawn to dusk. Don't worry if you can't do 12 to 14 miles a day at the start. Most can't. Eventually, with conditioning, you'll increase your mileage. Your pace will also fluctuate depending on the terrain—be prepared for single-digit and 20-plus-mile days alike. Leisurely hikers will have to keep

Section-Hiking: Another Option

Thru-hiking is a serious commitment of time and money. Truth is, many of us are unable or unwilling to justify taking six months out of our "real lives" to do it. Others take the plunge, only to be sidelined by injury or simple discouragement. Take heart—all is not lost.

Section-hiking offers another way to complete the trail, by tackling it in sections over a period of years. One of the A.T.'s youngest section-hikers started as a 3-year-old and completed the trail at age 15.

Set your sights high, keep planning, and remember—the trail is there when you're ready.

an eye on the weather, as snow becomes a factor in late fall.

Hiking with a partner or a group also changes the dynamics of a hike, as the slowest member often sets the pace. You may feel pressure to either downshift or keep up, depending on your own relative fitness. Differing interests or personality conflicts only exacerbate the situation. That said, sharing a thru-hike has distinct advantages, including companionship, pooled finances and resources, and safety. Predetermine your compatibility when choosing a hiking partner.

Keep in mind that averages are misleading, as few thru-hikers remain on the trail more than six consecutive days. Thus, a hiker who takes every seventh day off to pick up food, check mail, bathe, recuperate, and call home will have to walk 14 miles per day to maintain a 12-mile-a-day average over six months. That doesn't even take into account such variables as conditioning, terrain, weather, and available daylight. For instance, Shenandoah's gentle slopes and well-groomed footpath make long-distance days a breeze, and in summer you'll have about 16 hours of daylight in which to log miles. Farther north, New Hampshire's steep White Mountains and lack of switchbacks will test even the fittest hiker.

Fortunately, six months is a lot of time—enough time to start slowly during the first few weeks, work yourself into shape, then pick up the pace on less-strenuous sections. Above all, remind yourself that this is *your* hike. Set your own pace, and leave your finish date flexible, and it will be a successful one.

Which Direction?

Your chosen direction of travel will determine the nature of the entire thru-hike, from the departure date to pace, terrain, and climate. Refer to the "Departures & Arrivals" chart on page 16 for average daily mileages required to complete the trail within the typical season.

Do keep in mind seasonal averages with regard to hours of daylight. In Harpers Ferry, West Virginia, for example, daylight averages 13 hours in March, peaks at 16 hours in June and July, then drops back to 13 hours in September. An optimistic way to regard these averages is that, even on the shortest days, if you were to walk all day, you'd only have to hike one mile an hour—a stroll in the park.

Northbound

Springer to Katahdin (*GA>ME* in trail-register jargon) is the direction most thru-hikers travel. The first day of spring, usually March 20, is the romantic starting date, though Mother Nature is no respecter of romance. Snow and ice storms linger through April at higher elevations in Georgia, North Carolina, and Tennessee.

Northbounders must keep one seasonal deadline in mind: Katahdin, in Maine's Baxter State Park, closes to overnight hikers on October 15—earlier if weather conditions are especially harsh. Violators of this closure are subject to a court summons and fine, equipment seizure, and permanent revocation of park privileges. Also remember that fall days in Maine are quite short. The average northbound hiker must reach Harpers Ferry by mid-July. If you're still in Pennsylvania in mid-August, you definitely won't make it.

ATC strongly encourages would-be northbound thru-hikers to use its voluntary, on-line registration system to help determine their starting date. The system lets you see how many are planning to start on a given date, in the hope that people will spread the crunch out more to relieve pressure on themselves and the Trail's resources.

Sample 180-Day South-North Thru-Hiking Schedule

	MILES	DAYS	AVERAGE	COMMENTS
Springer to Damascus	469	46	10.2	Weeks to get into good hiking form while negotiating roller-coaster hills in the southern Appalachians.
Damascus to Waynesboro	392	33	11.9	Yes, you're in good hiking form, but the Blue Ridge terrain remains a challenge.
Waynesboro to North Adams	731	48	15.2	You'll hit your stride while crossing more level mid-Atlantic terrain on long summer days.
North Adams to Glencliff	198	15	13.2	Despite steeper terrain in the Green Mountains and New Hampshire, you press forward in top hiking form.
Glencliff to Caratunk	248	25	9.9	The A.T.'s most demanding climbs slow you down, as do possible nutritional deficits and shorter days.
Caratunk to Katahdin	151	13	11.6	Never mind the steep, muddy terrain and short fall days—they can't stop your legs of steel.
TOTALS	**2,189**	**180**	**12.1**	

To ease seasonal pressures, some northbound hikers decide to "flip-flop" (see next page) by late summer, driving or flying ahead to Katahdin, then hiking south on the trail to where they left off. But, don't wait too late to decide—fall weather in the White Mountains can be worse than Maine's, and the Appalachian Mountain Club's White Mountain huts start closing in September.

Southbound

A smaller pack of thru-hikers sets out southbound each year, typically after the spring muddy season and early-summer insect hatches. Trail restrictions at Baxter State Park prevent southbounders from starting from Katahdin before mid-May, and weather can delay the trail opening up to a month.

Southbound thru-hikes are traditionally the domain of individualists, as you'll encounter few fellow hikers going in the same direction—with good reason. In late spring, New England can be cold and wet, and the woods swarm with voracious northern blackflies. If you consider such factors a challenge more than a deterrent, best of luck.

Southbounders typically encounter northbounders by Vermont or Massachusetts, by which time they've experienced the most challenging terrain the trail has to offer. Remember, though, that the trail never gets easy, only less hard.

Flip-Flopping & Leapfrogging

Not everyone can (or wants to) start from Springer in March or April with the mass of northbound thru-hikers. Fewer still choose to battle the hatch of late-spring blackflies in Maine or wait for the more insect-free months of June or July to start south. A hiker wishing to avoid either scenario might consider flip-flopping (hiking a section of the trail in one direction, then returning to the starting point and hiking the opposite direction to trail's end) or leapfrogging (splitting the hike into more than two segments to capitalize on seasonal advantages regarding temperatures, insects, and other factors). ATC encourages flip-flopping to reduce impacts and overcrowding in the South, especially if the voluntary registration system at <www.appalachiantrail.org> is telling you March is just plain *jammed*.

A flip-flopper might start from Harpers Ferry in May, hike north to Katahdin, return to Harpers Ferry, then continue south to Springer with the southbounders. A leapfrogger might start at Springer in mid-April, hike north to Harpers Ferry, leapfrog to Great Barrington, Massachusetts, hike north to Katahdin, then return to Great Barrington, and hike south to Harpers Ferry.

Departures & Arrivals

DEPARTURE PLACE/TIME	AVERAGE MILES/DAY	ARRIVAL PLACE/TIME
SOUTH TO NORTH		
Springer / March	12	Katahdin / Sept.
Springer / April	18	Katahdin / Aug.
Springer / April	14	Katahdin / Sept.
Springer / April	12	Katahdin / Oct.
Springer / May	14	Katahdin / Oct.
NORTH TO SOUTH		
Katahdin / May	12	Springer / Nov.
Katahdin / June	18	Springer / Oct.
Katahdin / June	14	Springer / Nov.
Katahdin / June	12	Springer / Dec.
Katahdin / July	14	Springer / Dec.

Note: *Hiker access to Katahdin is restricted from mid-October to mid-May.*

A list of alternative itineraries and other advice is available on the ATC Web site (<www.appalachiantrail.org>) under Hiking.

Where to Stay

Some would-be thru-hikers try to plan every stop along the trail. Like the proverbial military strategy, such detailed itineraries rarely survive first contact with the enemy. However, plotting your daily progress will raise valid logistical questions: How often will you pitch your tent? Will you camp outside shelters with other hikers or opt for remote sites? When will you bunk in shelters? Will you stay at any motels or hostels? How much water should you carry? How many days will you rest from hiking?

A good alternative to daily plans is to plot a series of three- to five-day segments between points at which you expect to buy groceries or pick up mail drops. For instance, you might chart a leg from Springer Mountain to Neel Gap in four days, but omit specific camping/lodging plans. Instead, using your Shelters & Towns and Mail Drop Locations charts, rough out several possible camping/lodging scenarios.

Trail-town lodgings often book up on summer weekends and during popular festivals such as Trail Days in Damascus, Virginia (the weekend after Mother's Day). If you plan to meet someone in town during these times, reserve rooms in advance.

Whether or not you stay at shelters, they serve well as mileposts by which to gauge your progress along the trail, which has few current mileposts.

Shelter or Tent?

More than 250 backcountry shelters line the Appalachian Trail at varying intervals—about a day's hike or less apart for the average hiker. Sometimes called a lean-to in upper New England, the typical shelter has a metal or shingled roof, a wooden floor, and three walls (open to the elements on one side). Most lie near a creek or spring, and many (although not all) provide a nearby privy (toilet). Other than a few places that require reservations (including state and national parks and the White Mountain huts), hikers occupy A.T. shelters on a first-come, first-served basis; thru-hikers have no priority. Many shelters are adjacent to semideveloped campsites to better manage the impacts on the land.

Shelters are among the best places to keep dry in wet weather. Many

Leave No Trace

Volunteers spend considerable time and effort to build and maintain shelters. Please leave the structures and grounds clean and in good repair. Also refrain from cutting trees for firewood—use only downed wood. *And please do NOT whip out that Sharpie and tag shelters and signs; it could not be more rude and disrespectful of the A.T. and other hikers.* (P.S. to those who do: When you post that I-am-a-vandal selfie on line, law enforcement *is* watching.)

In areas that allow dispersed camping, choose either a well-worn site or one showing no signs of prior use. Avoid lightly used sites, as they may recover if left alone. Set up tents on durable surfaces, such as dead leaves or grass, well apart from each other and at least 70 feet from any water source.

For more information, see the Leave No Trace guidelines on page 94.

hikers stop by to socialize and scan the registers for comments and advice from fellow thru-hikers. Shelters also concentrate overnight traffic, reducing hiker impact on other trail sections.

On the downside, shelters are sometimes dirty and rodent-infested, and they can quickly get crowded, particularly in bad weather. Oftentimes, the distance between shelters is inconvenient—for example, if you're up for a 15-mile day, and target shelters are either a 10- or 20-mile hike from your starting point.

Designated campsites also line the trail at varying intervals. Sites usually lie on flat, clear ground near a water source; few provide a privy. To reduce hiker impact, some campsites (particularly in New England) offer wooden tent platforms on which you can pitch and tie down a freestanding tent. A few sites in heavily used areas require considerable upkeep by trail clubs, and consequently a nominal fee ($9 or less) is charged.

Some sections, notably the national forests in Georgia, North Carolina, Tennessee, Virginia, and Vermont, allow dispersed camping, leaving you to camp more or less where you like, at specified distances from trails and water sources. *At such sites, be especially careful to leave no trace.*

Given the A.T. shelter system, not to mention in-town hostels and motels, a tent may seem like unnecessary baggage for a thru-hike. But, despite the quaint trail adage, "There's always room in the shelter for one more person during a rainstorm," shelters do fill up, sometimes to the point that everyone must sleep on their sides. In the event of such crowds, rain, or a cold snap, the tent becomes your sanctuary. While shelters are largely unoccupied in summer, you won't be alone—mosquitoes, blackflies, and no-see-ums lie in wait for open-air campers. A tent offers respite from such feeding frenzies. A tent is also welcome when you arrive at a particularly beautiful spot (such as North Carolina's Max Patch) and decide to stay a few hours or overnight. Finally, if you hurt yourself, a tent will serve as shelter until help arrives.

Before you begin your thru-hike, learn to pitch and repack your tent in the rain while keeping the rest of your gear dry (it takes practice). Fold up the wet tent last and hang it from your pack.

Caution: Starting Early

While some northbound hikers start in February, they tempt fate in doing so, as snow and ice storms regularly hit the southern Appalachians in winter. Day hiking in bad weather is hard enough. Imagine spending several weeks in the cold with a wet tent, sleeping bag, and clothes. In recent years, long spells of bad weather have knocked many early birds off the trail.

Winter thru-hikes of the A.T. have only been attempted a few times, with good reason. It's very difficult and extremely dangerous. Temperatures plummet, snowdrifts are deep, water sources freeze, and stores, lodgings, and other services often close. You'll be alone for weeks at a time. Only very experienced hikers should even consider a winter thru-hike.

Weather

Starting on page 20 is a regional breakdown of typical weather conditions in spring, summer, and fall. For planning purposes, the trail has been divided

Neither Rain nor Snow...

Extreme weather conditions call for sound planning. In the Appalachians, storms generally come from the west. By simply watching cloud speed and direction, you'll rarely be surprised by storms. Here are other helpful tips:

Elevation—Weather at higher elevations is highly changeable, presenting hikers with unique challenges.

First, warm air cools as it rises into the mountains, losing about 3.5 to 4 degrees for every 1,000 feet of elevation gained, so temperatures in the mountains may be considerably lower than in the valleys. That elevation/temperature gradient also means that ridges are often socked in with clouds, fog, and rain. Keep those factors in mind when considering weather reports.

Snow—Snow and ice storms persist into April at higher elevations. Winter clothes and rain gear are a must, as temperatures can plummet quickly. Heavy snows have stranded thru-hikers in the past. If the forecast looks grim, be ready to ration food and wait out the storm in a shelter. In frigid conditions, a lightweight Mylar blanket may just save your life.

Rain—Intense spring showers are common and can turn the trail into a muddy mess. Shelters offer refuge from the damp. Be sure to change into dry clothes at your first opportunity, to ward off hypothermia. Let boots air-dry thoroughly. Rainy periods can also dampen a hiker's enthusiasm. Keep your spirits up by waiting out the worst of the storm. Read a good book, have a leisurely breakfast, then get going. If your route crosses any streams, beware of flood conditions.

Lightning—Lakes and ponds, open ridges, and mountaintops—all veritable lightning magnets—predominate along the Appalachian Trail. According to NOAA statistics, most strikes occur on late afternoons in summer. Given warning, head for the nearest shelter.

If you are caught in the open, shed all metal objects, including external-frame packs, tools, and hiking poles. Leave high ground immediately, keep away from trees or other prominent features, and minimize your contact with the ground (crouching works best). Groups of hikers should spread out. If someone is struck by lightning, be prepared to administer CPR.

Drought—In drought conditions, rainfall is sparse, temperatures remain high, and springs slow to a trickle or stop altogether. The greatest concern is having enough drinking water on hand to ward off dehydration. A hydration backpack is a godsend in such conditions. If caught short on supply, consider hiking off-trail to reliable springs (check your map). You can usually find water by heading down a water-sculpted gorge or ravine. When you do find water, drink as much as you can (at least a quart), and fill your canteen or other water container. The extra weight is a small price to pay.

into three general climatic zones: south (Georgia, North Carolina, Tennessee, Virginia, West Virginia, and Maryland), middle (Pennsylvania, New Jersey, New York, Connecticut, and Massachusetts) and north (Vermont, New Hampshire, and Maine).

Use these guidelines to assess gear and clothing requirements, but be aware they are broad generalizations—if nothing else, weather is unpredictable, especially in the mountains. Conditions can change fast, and a hiker must be prepared for the worst. At the very least, always carry rain gear, as hypothermia (page 52) is a real risk in any region year-round.

Average Monthly High/Low Temperatures & Precipitation Along the A.T.

LOCATION	ELEV. (FEET)	JANUARY TEMP	JANUARY PREC	FEBRUARY TEMP	FEBRUARY PREC	MARCH TEMP	MARCH PREC	APRIL TEMP	APRIL PREC	MAY TEMP	MAY PREC
Blairsville, Ga.	1,917	52 / 27	5.4	54 / 29	5.6	60 / 33	5.7	70 / 41	4.4	77 / 49	4.1
Clingmans Dome, Tenn.	6,643	35 / 19	7.0	35 / 18	8.2	39 / 24	8.2	49 / 34	6.5	57 / 43	6.0
Hot Springs, N.C.	1,480	51 / 31		52 / 32		60 / 37		70 / 44		78 / 53	
Watauga Dam, Tenn.	1,760	49 / 29		52 / 30		55 / 32		68 / 41		77 / 52	
Burkes Garden, Va.	3,300	42 / 23	4.0	43 / 23	3.6	51 / 29	4.6	62 / 38	3.7	70 / 45	4.1
Shenandoah National Park (Big Meadows), Va.	3,535	39 / 20	3.3	40 / 21	3.0	47 / 26	4.0	59 / 37	4.2	67 / 46	4.5
Hagerstown, Md.	560	41 / 25	2.7	44 / 27	2.6	51 / 31	3.5	63 / 40	3.0	74 / 50	3.7
Harrisburg, Pa.	338	38 / 24	2.6	41 / 26	2.3	49 / 31	3.2	64 / 42	3.0	75 / 52	4.1
Mt. Pocono, Pa.	1,915	31 / 16	3.5	32 / 15	3.0	51 / 22	4.0	54 / 34	1.2	66 / 43	4.2
Bear Mountain, N.Y.	1,300	32 / 18	3.4	33 / 19	2.8	43 / 27	3.9	55 / 38	4.3	66 / 48	5.3
Pittsfield, Mass.	1,170	30 / 12	3.0	32 / 15	2.9	39 / 22	3.1	53 / 33	4.1	66 / 43	4.1
Somerset, Vt.	2,080	27 / 7		28 / 5		36 / 14		48 / 27		61 / 38	
Mt. Washington, N.H.	6,288	14 / -4	8.5	15 / -2	7.3	21 / 6	9.4	29 / 16	8.4	42 / 30	8.2
Pinkham Notch, N.H.	2,000	27 / 7	4.7	28 / 7	4.0	35 / 16	5.7	47 / 28	4.7	61 / 39	5.0
Millinocket, Maine	405	25 / 6	5.6	29 / 7	5.4	38 / 18	4.4	50 / 30	3.7	64 / 40	3.1

Temp = degrees F

Prec = inches rain
(1" rain may = 10" snow during winter)

Not all recording stations report precipitation. Due to elevation differences, the above-listed high and low temperatures may not be representative of those encountered along the Appalachian Trail. To approximate temperatures

South

Late winter/spring—Expect low temperatures and snow, especially at higher elevations. Heavy snowstorms are possible through March, sometimes making trails impassable. Daytime temperatures rise by late April, although nights often remain quite cold. This also marks a rainy period. By May, temperatures warm dramatically, with daytime highs in the 70s and sometimes 80s. Nights are comfortably cool.

Summer—Summer days down south are hot and humid, often reaching the high 90s and occasionally topping 100. Consider sending home that winter sweater for a few months. Rain showers are infrequent and typically

| JUNE | | JULY | | AUGUST | | SEPTEMBER | | OCTOBER | | NOVEMBER | | DECEMBER | |
TEMP	PREC	TEMP	PREC	TEMP	PREC	TEMP	PREC	TEMP	PREC	TEMP	PREC	TEMP	PREC
83 / 57	3.8	85 / 61	5.3	85 / 60	4.4	80 / 54	3.4	71 / 42	3.2	61 / 32	3.4	53 / 27	5.0
63 / 49	6.9	65 / 53	8.3	64 / 52	6.8	60 / 47	5.1	53 / 38	5.4	42 / 28	6.4	37 / 21	7.3
85 / 61		87 / 64		86 / 63		82 / 58		72 / 47		60 / 36		51 / 31	
83 / 59		86 / 62		86 / 62		81 / 55		71 / 46		57 / 33		48 / 27	
76 / 52	4.5	79 / 56	4.6	78 / 55	4.3	73 / 48	3.3	64 / 38	2.8	51 / 29	2.9	43 / 23	3.5
74 / 54	4.6	76 / 57	4.9	75 / 56	6.2	69 / 50	4.9	60 / 41	5.1	49 / 30	3.7	39 / 22	3.5
82 / 59	3.5	86 / 63	3.5	84 / 61	3.8	78 / 54	2.8	67 / 43	2.5	53 / 34	2.9	42 / 26	2.8
83 / 61	3.2	87 / 65	3.4	85 / 63	3.4	78 / 56	2.6	67 / 45	2.7	52 / 35	3.0	41 / 26	2.9
74 / 51	4.9	77 / 56	5.2	76 / 55	4.8	69 / 48	4.7	60 / 39	4.6	46 / 28	3.7	33 / 18	3.8
75 / 57	4.1	79 / 63	5.7	77 / 61	4.0	70 / 54	3.5	60 / 44	3.4	47 / 33	4.6	35 / 22	4.1
75 / 52	4.4	79 / 56	4.7	78 / 55	3.5	69 / 47	4.2	59 / 37	3.0	46 / 29	4.0	33 / 17	3.4
70 / 47		75 / 51		73 / 49		66 / 42		56 / 33		41 / 23		29 / 12	
50 / 39	8.4	54 / 43	8.0	53 / 42	8.1	46 / 35	8.6	36 / 24	7.7	28 / 14	10.5	19 / 2	8.8
69 / 48	5.0	74 / 53	4.6	72 / 51	4.4	64 / 44	5.0	55 / 35	5.2	41 / 24	5.7	29 / 11	4.8
73 / 49	3.6	79 / 56	3.8	77 / 53	3.7	68 / 45	2.9	57 / 35	3.6	42 / 27	5.2	29 / 12	4.9

for the A.T. relative to the nearest recording station, subtract 3.5 degrees Fahrenheit per 1,000 feet of elevation. To find trail elevations nearest the towns listed above, consult the Appalachian Trail Data Book.

brief—perfect opportunities to stop by a shelter for a long lunch or a nap. Nights remain fairly cool and pleasant.

Fall—Temperatures drop by October, with daytime highs between 60 and 70 degrees and nighttime lows occasionally below freezing. Precipitation is minimal, enabling more comfortable hiking. Beware of hunters, however, particularly if you're southbound. Check ATC's Web site (<www.appalachiantrail.org>) for local hunting seasons. In season, remain on the trail and wear lots of blaze orange for visibility.

Middle

Late winter/spring—March and April aren't the best months to hike through this region, as prevailing conditions are wet and muddy, with snow possible well into April. Biting insects hatch in swarms in April and May, making life along the trail a challenge. Temperatures climb into the 50s, but reliable warmth doesn't arrive till late May or June.

Summer—Although bugs persist through August, hikers with insect repellent and tents survive. Daytime highs range from the 80s into the humid 90s, with cooler nights, although nights at lower elevations can be uncomfortably warm. Rain is common, so adequate rain gear is necessary. If rainfall is below normal, look for seasonal springs along the ridgeline.

Fall—Temperatures cool by November, and bug populations drop off. Generally, this is a great time to hike, as changing leaves offer a spectrum of vivid colors from mid- to late October. Nights are chilly, however, with frosts likely by October.

North

Late winter/spring—Forget it! This is a terrible time to hike the northern Appalachians. Snowstorms and heavy rains are common, particularly in the mountains. Once the ground thaws, the A.T. becomes a nearly impassable bog. Nights are bitter cold. To make matters worse, late spring is hatching season for the infamous northern blackfly—a truly loathsome companion. Most A.T. authorities suggest waiting at least until June to start a thru-hike from Katahdin. Even then, challenging conditions make it a difficult starting point.

Summer—Summer is relatively pleasant, despite persistent bugs. Days are generally in the 70s, sometimes in the 80s, and occasionally in the 90s. Warm clothing is a must for chilly nights and mornings. Bear in mind that extreme weather is possible year-round, including snow and below-freezing conditions, particularly in New Hampshire's White Mountains. Proper rain gear is required.

Fall—Fall is often a pleasant time to hike, with cool days, chilly nights, and beautiful foliage displays in late September and early October. Insects disappear, but rains are frequent. Snow is a definite possibility in September. Mid-October heralds the arrival of winter, closing the trail to Katahdin.

Chapter ☑ Worksheet

**Tear out the Thru-Hike Budget worksheet
on page 81 and estimate expenses
as you read through this
and the following chapters.**

If time is the biggest practical consideration when planning a thru-hike, then money runs a close second. While it's a bargain in comparison to many other six-month jaunts, a thru-hike isn't exactly cheap (see "Dollars & Sense" on page 24). Many a thru-hiker has been forced from the trail because he or she ran out of money.

A thru-hike is most affordable when you're just out of school, with no debt, no lease or mortgage, and a few thousand bucks in the bank from mowing lawns and waiting tables. It's most costly when you're in mid-career, with dependents, debts to pay, and commitments to keep. If you're retired, with few financial obligations, money may not be the most pressing concern.

Living expenses are minimal on the trail. Once you've bought all the necessary gear and clothing, your only expenses will be food and replacement gear, although you'll want spare cash for the occasional town visit. Hiking partners and groups can share supplies, further reducing travel expenses (not to mention pack weight).

When budgeting discretionary costs, ask yourself: How much am I willing to spend on good food? How many times will I stay at an inn or lodge or have dinner in a nice restaurant? Will I go whitewater rafting?

You could hike the trail on a shoestring, but why deprive yourself? Work another year at your job, then hike and finish with money left in the bank.

Plan to earn the money in advance. It's very difficult to complete a thru-hike while job-hopping along the trail, few employers will pay you to thru-hike, and financing your adventure through such projects as charity walkathons, guidebook writing, or documentary film-making will seriously constrain your hiking experience. With good planning, a thru-hike will offer a four- to six-month respite from money concerns and outside obligations.

Dollars & Sense

Following are a few financial pointers to keep in mind:

▷ **Food, lodging, and incidental expenses run about $1.75–$2.70 per mile for a reasonably frugal (although not uncomfortable) thru-hike. Allow yourself $595 to $985 per month, including transportation to trailheads. A recent survey of thru-hikers found about a third spending $3,000–$5,000 and another third in the $5,000–$7,000 range. Partners cut the cost below $5,000 each.**

▷ **The average costs for trailside hostels and hotels/motels are about $20–$35 and $45–$150, respectively.**

▷ **Have more money in reserve than you think you'll need. Even small indulgences can add up over five to seven months.**

▷ **As you budget, calculate gear and transportation costs separately from the cost of food, lodging, and incidental expenses.**

▷ **Need to cut costs while on the trail? Limit your discretionary spending. Don't stay in town—only visit to pick up supplies, do laundry, and clean up. Also resist the temptation to accompany fellow hikers to restaurants, bars, and lodging.**

▷ **A few inns and stores along the trail will exchange food or lodging for a few hours of work. AMC's White Mountain huts and campsites may also negotiate "work for stay."**

▷ **Don't let financial obligations back home ruin your hike. Many banks now offer automatic bill payment, and some provide online banking services you can access from your phone, public libraries, and Internet cafés. Have a trusted family member or friend monitor your balances and pay any bills you can't prepay or pay automatically.**

Trail Funds

Whether to carry cash on the trail is a subject of debate among thru-hikers. Some pack large amounts of cash, while others carry very little, opting instead to bring an ATM card or debit card for intermittent withdrawals. Don't send cash from home through the mail, as it may get lost or stolen.

A good compromise is to carry enough cash to cover unexpected supplies, lodging, meals, or shuttles into town. Don't carry so much cash that your hike will be threatened if you drop your wallet or a thief makes off with your backpack. Stash a few bills in a secure location (jacket pocket, eyeglasses pouch), just in case.

Debit-card withdrawals and credit-card advances may be the easiest way to get cash on the trail. Today, even small-town banks and convenience stores have ATMs, and most post offices will return up to $50 cash back if you use a debit card to buy stamps. Be prepared to show a photo ID, even if your hiker self (weight loss, new beard) bears little resemblance—most banks along the A.T. serve hikers regularly and understand.

A service charge (and much higher interest fees) will be billed to your credit card for cash advances. ATM withdrawals incur a transaction fee of a few dollars, even if it's your home bank. If you don't already have one, consider opening an account with a large national bank that has branches all along the A.T.; that might reduce fees if banks are continuously adjusting those. Arrange to pay credit-card bills in full each month to avoid finance charges, which can mount up.

Banks usually refuse to cash personal checks, unless you have an account with them, and most stores along the trail won't accept personal checks from out-of-town banks. Most stores that accept credit cards also accept debit cards. As debit cards draw money directly from your bank account, keep especially good track of them and never write your PIN on the card.

Traveler's checks are widely accepted in trail towns. Denominations of $20 are easier for smaller establishments to cash. Some hikers mail themselves traveler's checks along the way.

Chapter ☑ Checklist

A removable Gear Checklist on page 82 is divided into three sections:

Essential—equipment you must bring on a thru-hike.

Useful—gear you may find handy but could survive without.

Optional—material you don't need but might enjoy.

The list is intended solely as a guideline—what another hiker considers useful you may find essential, provided you're willing to shoulder the extra weight.

Few areas of thru-hike planning perplex the uninitiated more than gear selection. First-timers often pack either way too much or way too little gear. Of course, unless you've hiked long distances before, how would you know what to expect?

You're in luck. Several books offer general overviews, among them Triple-Crowner Andrew Skurka's *The Ultimate Hiker's Gear Guide: Tools and Techniques to Hit the Trail*, published by National Geographic Books. Many A.T.-specific advice books also are available, although gear-advice Web sites are today's best sources of good information about current gear. Also valuable, if planning ahead, are venues such as mid-May Trail Days in Damascus, Va., and the annual ALDHA Gathering in October, because you can talk to current hikers, see their gear, and attend workshops. Outfitters on or close to the trail or with past thru-hikers as employees are also excellent sources of advice.

Now, your equipment won't do the hiking for you, so don't get too obsessed about it. Each year, people successfully thru-hike the A.T. in cheap, no-frills gear, while others outfitted in pricey, high-tech setups drop out in their first two weeks on the trail. Gear doesn't make the hiker.

That said, proper gear is invaluable, and thru-hikers talk about it constantly—one-upping each other with clever innovations and eying one another's backpacks and boots the way car buffs size up cylinder blocks. The right equipment and a good fit will make your hike safer and more comfortable, boosting your odds of success.

Following is a basic breakdown of gear needs and wants. For more information and a list of helpful resources, flip to the appendix (page 55) or visit ATC online at <www.appalachiantrail.org>.

Footwear

Gearheads diverge on which *boots* work best, but today the norm is a light-weight, trail-runner-type *shoe*—perhaps up to midweight.

The primary consideration is a good fit. When you try on boots or shoes in the store, wait until later in the day when your feet are swollen, and be sure to wear a pair of appropriate hiking socks (see Socks below). The long hours you will be putting in, hour after hour with weight on your back, will affect your feet, so think ahead: Buy a half-size larger than you might choose otherwise.

Brands, styles, and materials run the gamut. Midweights straddle comfort and support; breathable lightweights make 20-mile days bearable. Your own preference will be a compromise between comfort and durability. Prices typically range between $75 and $300. You'll pay less for disposable budget boots and much more for custom-made models, rarely seen on the A.T. today.

No matter how much you spend, one pair of footwear will not carry you the entire 2,189-plus miles without repair or replacement. Soles simply wear out. Be prepared to buy another from the trail.

Once you're out on the trail, be kind to your footwear. At the end of the day, remove debris from the soles and clean off any accumulated mud. Prop inserts upright in each, pull out the tongues, and let them air dry overnight. Keep them away from fire rings and other heat sources.

Socks

Socks are your first line of defense against blisters and other foot problems. Pack a few pairs to last you through fall.

Avoid cotton, which absorbs water and perspiration but is slow to dry, increasing friction and opening the door to blisters or frostbite in cold weather. Instead, look for socks made of fast-drying wool or synthetics (polypropylene, acrylic, Cool Max).

Some hikers also wear thin silk or polypropylene sock liners, which fit inside one's primary socks, further reducing friction.

Gaiters

A nice accessory for hiking in rain or snow, gaiters fit over your boots and lower legs, keeping your socks and feet mostly dry. Tall gaiters also keep your legs warm and offer protection from underbrush and the ticks that thrive there. Gaiters also enable hikers to keep to midtrail no matter the conditions, cutting down on soil erosion. Best of all, they keep pebbles, twigs, and leaves out of your shoes.

Backpack

With design advances and a better grasp of ergonomics, gear manufacturers now turn out backpacks to fit hikers of every size and shape. Suspension frames, hip belts, and load-lifter straps leave you free to enjoy the trail

---

Breaking in New Boots

Once you buy a pair of boots, if you go that route, break them in slowly on short hikes. While lightweight models are often comfy after a few hours on your feet, seldom-seen leather boots may take several weeks of conditioning and wear to fit your feet. Shortcut the process by wearing them around the house or while mowing the lawn. If rough spots remain, have your outfitter or shoe-repair shop work its magic.

without breaking your back beneath an ill-fitting pack or Army-surplus rucksack.

The two main pack categories are internal frame or external frame. Internal-frame packs offer a narrow profile and padded fit, as well as an integrated sleeping-bag compartment. Drawbacks include fewer external pockets, hindering access to gear. An internal-frame pack also rests directly on one's back, making it a bit warm in summer.

The somewhat bulkier external-frame packs offer plenty of outside pockets, making gear access a snap, but are rare on today's trail. The frame usually features metal stands that keep the pack out of the muck when placed on the ground. Because the pack rests off the back an inch or so, there's room for air to circulate and cool its wearer. External-frame packs are marginally harder to balance.

A decent, reliable external-frame pack will run you around $200, while internal-frame packs range from $240 up to $550.

When shopping for a pack, look for a carrying capacity between 3,000 and 4,000 cubic inches, more if you will be starting during winter conditions. Bring along a duffel bag filled with at least 25 pounds of "stuff"—ideally the gear you plan to bring. Once you've picked out a pack, see if the duffel will fit, then stroll a few circuits of the store to gauge fit and comfort.

Pack Cover

Despite the best water-resistant fabrics and coatings, rain will find its way into your pack unless you use a waterproof pack cover. Many manufacturers sell custom covers to fit their packs. If you use an external-frame pack, be sure the cover is big enough to protect gear strapped on the outside. On clear days, hang the cover from your pack to dry.

Tent & Tarp

Functional, free-standing, strong, and bug-proof, today's lightweight tents range in weight from just more than a pound for a one-person bivy to around six pounds for a two-person tent with rainfly. Collapsible shock-cord poles and plastic clips enable quick setup and breakdown—a welcome feature when it rains. No-see-um netting thwarts insects and allows breezes to cool the tent in summer. A three-season tent should keep out most weather you'll face.

Although a rainfly will shield you from precipitation, also treat all seams and the floor with sealant, often provided by the tent manufacturer. Consider resealing the seams midway through your hike. A lightweight tarp or custom plastic "footprint" will protect the tent floor and offer an additional moisture barrier.

For more elbow room, consider a compact two-person tent. Otherwise, opt for a lightweight one-person model. Prices for the latter range between $100 and $200.

If you are traveling with a partner or group, consider sharing a larger tent to save collective pack weight. Keep in mind, however, that you'll be "roommates" for several months—be sure you're compatible.

Tied off on neighboring trees, a stowable hammock is an alternative to sleeping on the ground. To protect against biting insects, shroud the hammock in a length of no-see-um netting. A tarp offers protection from the rain. Try this at home several evenings before you commit.

Tent-Repair Kit

Inexpensive and fairly compact, a tent-repair kit may come in handy. A typical kit contains ripstop fabric patches, sealant, and aluminum pole ferrules (joints). Duct tape will work in a pinch.

Sleeping Bag

While expensive ($150 to $350), a down-filled mummy bag offers several advantages over synthetic-fill bags. Down is lightweight and warm and can be stuffed into a pack, saving loads of space. Its main disadvantage is that, should it get wet, it will lose *all* insulating properties until it dries, which can take a long time.

Synthetic-fill bags are bulkier and heavier, but they can get damp or even soggy and still keep you warm (although maybe not comfortably warm). Since the trail can be a rather wet place, this is an important consideration. They're also cheaper ($100 or less).

Sleeping bags are rated according to air temperatures you'll face on the trail. If you sleep cold, look for a bag rated about 10 degrees colder than you expect. A washable bag liner may add a degree or two of warmth and keep your bag clean. Long sizes are available for tall (6-foot-plus) hikers, and couples can purchase bags that zip together—a nice way to share the warmth.

Sleeping Pad

Many thru-hikers swear by Therm-a-Rest pads, lightweight self-inflating mattresses that cushion sleepers from the hard ground or shelter floor. Prices start at about $60.

Lightweight, foam sleeping pads also work well and cost much less ($15 to $20).

Hardy souls make a bed from pine needles or loose soil. Picture yourself in this situation (better yet, try it several evenings at home). If you still think you can do without a sleeping pad, great—you've saved money and weight.

Stuff Sack

Usually made of ripstop nylon, with a toggled draw cord, stuff sacks are terrific for storing gear. Hikers using internal-frame packs find that stuff sacks enable them to better balance their loads. If you have a bulky, synthetic-fill

Choosing Brands

Hard-core hikers are often passionate about gear and fiercely loyal to their favorite brands, but brands and styles come and go. How does one distinguish the deals from the duds? A good starting point is one of the following online hiking forums:

▷ <www.whiteblaze.net>—This "Community of Appalachian Trail Enthusiasts" features several gear discussion threads under its Forums link.

▷ <www.trailjournals.com>—A collection of section- and thru-hiker journals, each offering personalized gear lists; follow the TrailForums link to read gear tips and post your own nagging questions.

For further links, flip to the appendix (page 57).

sleeping bag, a compression sack will keep it more manageable.

Stuff sacks also make excellent bear bags (see "Bears & Food," page 40).

Nylon Cord

Another versatile item marketed these days as para-cord, nylon cord can be used as a clothesline, binding, shoelaces, or an emergency belt (as you shrink out of your once-snug pants). Pack a 40- to 50-foot length to suspend a bear bag from a tree branch.

Clothing

Packing suitable thru-hike clothing is extremely important. The old adage, "When in doubt, leave it out," could put you at risk on the trail, particularly if you face cold, wet days without adequate insulating layers. At higher elevations, hypothermia (page 52) is a year-round danger. So, while that bulky wool sweater might be a space hog, it might also save your life.

Northbounders will need warm clothing from Springer Mountain up past Mt. Rogers in southern Virginia. At that point, forward it by mail drop to perhaps Cheshire, Massachusetts (nights can get nippy in northern New England, even in August). Southbounders should hold on to their warm clothing through Vermont, then send it ahead to, say, Harpers Ferry, West Virginia (ATC headquarters).

Layering is the key to extending your wardrobe's usefulness. Wear two, three, or even four layers at once for warmth in the mornings and evenings. While hiking, you can shed a layer or two to cool off, then replace layers as needed to keep warm during breaks. Experiment with various combinations until you find your ideal mix.

As with socks, avoid cotton, as it retains moisture and is slow to dry, opening the door to hypothermia in cold weather. Wool (especially merino), silk, and lightweight synthetic fabrics (Capilene, Cool Max, Dri-release, polypropylene, Thermax, *etc.*) are excellent insulators and wick moisture away from a wearer's skin to outer layers. Wool's drawbacks include its bulk and tendency to itch—wearing a synthetic base layer can solve the latter. Synthetics have two minor shortcomings: While generally strong and resilient, these materials wear down quickly at contact points (pack straps and hip belts). They also retain body odor and can get quite stinky after several days of wear (see "Sniff, Sniff..." on the next page), although manufacturers today routinely incorporate odor resistance.

Packing Tips

▷ **Ideally, a fully loaded pack should weigh no more than 35 pounds—some think much less. Less weight equals a faster pace.**

▷ **Reassess each piece of gear, and ask yourself whether you can do without it. You could always send it back from the trail, but why lug it along in the first place?**

▷ **Pack with accessibility in mind, putting seasonal items deep in your pack, while keeping everyday items close at hand.**

▷ **Keep a separate inventory list in an outside pocket of your backpack for easy reference.**

▷ **Before striking out on the A.T., field-test your full set-up on a shakedown hike in similar surroundings. Throw in a steep grade or two for good measure. Take the stairs!**

Starting from the bottom (so to speak), underwear should be breathable and comfortable. Men opt for wool boxers or synthetic briefs, while women choose synthetic briefs or hiking shorts with integrated liners and supportive sports bras. Close-fitting, synthetic long underwear is a must for the initial colder sections.

Wool and wicking synthetics are also the choice for mid-layer T-shirts, shorts, and pants, while insulating layers incorporate fleece into the mix for warm pullovers, sweaters, vests, and jackets. Pack a synthetic or fleece shirt/pants set to wear in camp while your hiking clothes air-dry.

Proper outer-layer clothing is perhaps most important to your comfort. The best rain gear strikes a balance between water resilience and breathability. While nylon/PVC ponchos and jackets do keep rain out, they trap sweat and heat, making for an unpleasant hike. Breathable Gore-Tex jackets and pants, on the other hand, offer comparable protection from the elements while letting air circulate to grateful skin. Look for a jacket with plenty of vents and zippers, adjustable openings, and an integrated hood.

Hat & Gloves

While your jacket's integrated hood will keep you dry, it won't keep your noggin warm on cold days. A good fleece hat or balaclava is mandatory gear, as up to 80 percent of total heat loss is through the head. Wear it to bed for a toasty night's sleep. Pack a lightweight pair of gloves or mittens to fend off frostbite.

In summer, a ball cap or wide-brimmed hat offers protection from the sun and rain. Southbounders should consider a blaze-orange cap as part of their hunting-season ensemble.

Bandanna

Bandannas are much more than fashionable doggie neckwear. Use them as a headband or hat, handkerchief, or emergency bandage. They're also useful for binding a broken pack frame or hanging fragile food items (fruit, bread) from your pack. The Original Buff® is a popular alternative.

Sunglasses & Eyeglasses

A must for winter hiking, sunglasses are welcome any bright day on an exposed ridgeline. Eyeglass wearers should bring a backup pair in case

Sniff, Sniff ...

A thru-hiker's wardrobe is bound to get a little ripe from time to time. If wildlife start to follow you, it may be time to take action. Here are a few tips to keep the stench to a minimum:

▷ **Rinse your clothes in the evening, especially socks and underwear; synthetics should dry by morning.**

▷ **If clothes are still wet in the morning, hang them securely from your backpack to dry as you hike.**

▷ **Air out boots each night and your sleeping bag each morning.**

▷ **Keep truly pungent clothes in a separate trash bag and launder in town.**

of damage or loss. Be sure to have your prescription handy should you need a replacement pair.

Hiking Stick/Trekking Poles

The vast majority of thru-hikers use a stick or pair of telescoping aluminum trekking poles ($50 and up). Proponents say staffs provide hikers with better footing and reduce the load on one's legs, saving overworked joints. They can also be used as lean-to supports or emergency splints or to fend off aggressive dogs.

Ecofriendly hikers add rubber tips to their poles to reduce soil damage and marks on trailside rocks. Critics claim that such supports merely add weight and slow them down. To determine your preference, borrow some, and give them a work-out.

Knife/Multitool

Virtually everyone carries a Swiss Army knife or multitool, some with useful miniature saw blades. Make sure the knife is sharp before you leave.

Thinking of carrying a machete? Save it for the Amazon.

Stove

Those who want to be pioneers and cook over an open fire will find that difficult on the trail, as well as *not* Leave No Trace-friendly. Usable wood is scarce near shelters, and any wood you do find is often damp. Furthermore, open fires are illegal in several states. Thus, the vast majority of thru-hikers carry a stove.

Many types are available—from Dad's old trunk-sized two-burner to ones that fit in your pocket. Look for one that is lightweight, compact, easy to use, and able to burn any type of fuel. Popular brands include Coleman, MSR, and Jetboil. The most expensive fuels, butane and propane, are clean-burning and can't spill, although you must pack out the empty cartridges, and butane doesn't work well below freezing. A recent thru-hiker survey found that half preferred nonrefillable canister stoves—easier to use but more expensive and wasteful. Other fuels include white gas (Coleman fuel) and kerosene. Consider purchasing a stove-repair kit, which contains spare stove parts and a cleaning tool.

One popular option is a lightweight can stove, made from a discarded soda can, perforated with air holes and fueled with denatured alcohol. Although you'll save money and a few ounces of pack weight, can stoves burn less efficiently. Surf the Web or ask your local outfitter for more information.

Matches/Lighter

Carry several packs of strike-anywhere matches in resealable plastic bags to keep them dry. Water- and windproof matches are also available. A cheap disposable lighter is another lightweight option, although the fuel may run out at an inopportune moment.

Cookware

To save weight, stick to the basics: a small aluminum pot and lid (go up one size if hiking with a partner), a spoon, and a wire-handled Sierra cup. The lid will cut down on cooking time and can double as your plate. Use your utility knife or multitool to open containers and cut food. A Sierra cup is also useful for scooping water from a shallow spring.

For cleanup, pack a nylon pot scrubber in a resealable plastic bag. Use potable water and a minimal amount of soap (see page 34).

Water Bag

A collapsible water bag—basically, a large plastic bladder in a nylon sleeve—is the perfect water tote. Virtually weightless when empty, these can hold up to five gallons, although half that is plenty for all your cooking/washing needs. You'll appreciate the large carrying capacity, especially when the nearest water source is a long downhill slog.

Water Filter/Purifier

While the clear water of natural springs and mountain streams may look tempting, drinking untreated water could sideline you for days or end your thru-hike altogether. (See "Health & Safety," page 51.)

Water-treatment options include iodine (tablets, crystals, or liquid), which works on bacteria but leaves a foul taste. Long-term iodine use also poses health risks, particularly to pregnant women and people with thyroid problems. Liquid chlorine dioxide is safer and more effective, but expensive over the long term. Simply boiling water for a few minutes is very effective but uses up lots of stove fuel, especially at higher elevations.

A growing number of hikers have turned to portable, hand-pumped filters and purifiers, especially the SteriPEN ultraviolet-light devices. Most filters screen out bacteria but not smaller viruses. One solution is to pretreat the water with iodine, then use a filter with carbon stages to remove most of the iodine. Purifiers combine filter stages and an element to neutralize bacteria and viruses. Make sure whatever filter/purifier you buy has a maximum porosity of 0.2 micron, which will filter out most bacteria.

Hydration System

At minimum, hikers should drink a gallon of water each day. A trusty quart water bottle can still do the trick, although you'll need to refill it often or use several bottles. A better option is an integrated hydration system.

Many backpacks now provide pockets for collapsible polyurethane water reservoirs, allowing hikers to sip from a demand valve without having to stop for a drink. When selecting a reservoir, or bladder, the bigger the better—up to 110 ounces (just shy of a gallon). Use only potable drinking water and regularly drain, clean, and dry the reservoir to prevent bacterial build-up.

Hikers complain that filters can be a chore to operate, clog easily, and require replacement cartridges over the course of a thru-hike. To prevent frequent clogging, use a prefilter to screen out sediment. Reusable ceramic filters can be cleaned many times before needing replacement, a desirable feature on a thru-hike.

Prices for such systems range broadly from about $30 to more than $200.

Flashlight/Headlamp

Every hiker should carry a light source, both for evening use and as a safety measure should you become lost or injured. Each member of a hiking team or group should have a light, in case you split up for some reason. Look for a lightweight, water-resistant model that will hold up to the trail and, more importantly, work at low temperatures.

Flashlights ($10 to $20 and up) are compact and allow you to direct light where needed. Water-resistant aluminum Mag lights are prized for their strength and compactness (an ounce or two, with batteries).

Almost all thru-hikers opt for headlamps ($20 to $40 and up) to keep their hands free, particularly when setting up camp in the dark or logging miles on cool summer nights. Those feature high-intensity lamps in a lightweight harness.

Pack enough spare batteries to last until your next planned town visit and be sure to pack out used batteries. You'll go through fewer batteries on long summer days.

Candle

If you have the energy to read at night, slow-burning candles will spare your flashlight batteries. Be sure to snuff out the candle before bedtime!

Whistle

Carry a whistle to signal others if you get lost or injured, especially if you're hiking solo.

Toilet Paper

"Mountain money" in thru-hiker jargon, toilet paper by the roll is a pain in the, ahem, to carry. Instead, peel off half-rolls and keep them dry in resealable plastic bags. Either bury used paper in a 6- to 8-inch deep "cathole" (see page 51) or pack out used paper in another, *well-marked* resealable bag. Do *not* burn used paper, as it poses a wildfire risk.

Plastic Garbage Bags

Useful for storing laundry and keeping clothing and other items separate and dry.

Resealable Plastic Bags

Indispensable for holding everything from snacks to soap.

Soap & Travel Towel

Make sure your soap is biodegradable and that you use it at least 200 feet from any water source (see Leave No Trace, page 94).

Dr. Bronner's liquid peppermint soap has brand-name cachet among thru-hikers. Although expensive (about $2.50 for 4 ounces), it is concentrated and can clean your pots, clothes, skin, and even your teeth. Other organic oils are available if the peppermint feels a bit too astringent.

A small, synthetic microfiber towel will dry quickly and take up very little room in your pack. Frequent rinsing and thorough drying should ward off the funkies.

Who You Callin' a Lightweight?

Lightweight hiking is based on the principle that less is more. While traditional long-distance hikers haul up to one-third their body weight in gear, lightweight (or ultralight) hikers typically tote packs weighing less than 30 pounds—some less than 10 pounds! Proponents point to several benefits, including dramatic increases in daily mileage (30 to 40 miles per day) and a reduction in stress-related injuries. By focusing less on gear, they hope to foster a closer bond with nature.

To achieve such light loads, hikers eschew bulky packs for frameless rucksacks, tents for tarps, boots for running shoes, and so on, shaving ounces wherever possible. Extreme measures include trimming the edges off maps and clipping labels from clothing. Popularized by such author/hikers as Ray Jardine and Colin Fletcher and boosted by advances in gear design, the practice has caught on.

Anyone considering this approach must bear in mind that limited gear means limited resources in adverse conditions. Be sure you are fit, err on the side of caution, and enroll in a wilderness first-aid course that addresses such setbacks.

Comb

A lightweight plastic comb will undo any trail tangles. Plus, you can combine a comb with a piece of paper to make a kazoo.

Toothbrush, Paste & Floss

Regular brushing is one aspect of civilization worth bringing to the trail, and your fellow hikers will be grateful. If you want to heed lightweight hikers' advice and saw off the handle to save a quarter-ounce, go for it, although a toothbrush without a handle is hard to use.

You'll find travel-sized toothpaste tubes in trail towns. To save an ounce or two of pack weight, you could use Dr. Bonner's peppermint soap—*soap* being the operative word. Baking soda also works well and doesn't taste as bad.

Also carry several yards of dental floss to keep your teeth and gums happy. Keep everything in a resealable plastic bag.

Sunscreen & Lip Balm

Long-term exposure to the elements can be hard on the skin. Be sure to pack sunscreen (minimum SPF 15) for those sunny stretches of the trail. Also, bring a tube of lip balm to save your lips from cracking due to cold, heat, sun, and wind.

Insect Repellent

Hikers vary widely in their susceptibility to biting insects, which along the trail include ticks, mosquitoes, no-see-ums, and blackflies. If those pariahs find you irresistible, DEET and permethrin remain your best defense.

Commercial repellent contains anywhere from 5 percent to 100 percent DEET. For deep-woods use, choose one with at least 20 percent to 30 percent concentration. Reapply as necessary during vigorous hiking, and keep it away from your eyes.

For use on clothing only, products containing permethrin will kill ticks on contact.

Natural repellents exist but can be more expensive and less effective.

First-Aid Kit

See page 54.

ID

Bring a driver's license or other photo ID to pick up mail-drop packages, cash personal checks, seek credit-card advances, or buy beer/wine on town days. It's also fun to show fellow thru-hikers what you looked like before the hike!

Camera

Know your camera and its needs, and pack accordingly, remembering that

---

Phone Home

Cellular-telephone coverage is rapidly improving along the A.T., and almost all hikers carry some model of "smartphone" and/ or tablet. Depending on battery life and recharging options, photos and calling home are still the primary uses, but use of "apps" is increasing. If you choose to carry one, please talk out of sound range of other hikers.

recharging will need to wait until town. Serious shutterbugs might throw in a pocket tripod, although a tree limb will work in a pinch.

Pack a portable battery-charger for town visits or spring for a compact, foldable solar battery charger or other portable recharging devices (an exploding market). Some accommodate digital-camera batteries.

Journal

On a thru-hike, your journal will serve as diary, planner, address book, sketchpad, friend, and therapist all wrapped into one. You can also share information with fellow hikers and, in years to come, regale your grandchildren with tales from the trail. Some hikers maintain their journals on line, directly (often from libraries) or *via* friends who post them. But, *please, avoid posting your whereabouts in real time for public viewing.*

Pen/Pencil

Pack a pen or pencil to update your journal, sign registers, leave notes for other hikers, write postcards, take down directions, and sign checks. Include a spare so you don't run out of ink/lead in the middle of a profound thought.

Postcards

Purchase the prestamped ones from post offices, and pack a handful so you can write to someone when inspired by a gorgeous view or quiet shelter. (Sure, you can "post" a modern way—and suck battery life.)

Trail Guides & Maps

Most thru-hikers carry either the *Appalachian Trail Thru-Hikers' Companion*—which includes tables of mileages between landmarks, road crossings, shelters, campsites, and towns, along with elevation profiles, trail-town information and listings—or the differently formatted *Appalachian Trail Guide,* also annually updated. Good topographic maps should be considered essential safety equipment—the A.T. is marked well, but, if you need to get off in a hurry, give a location to someone coming to help your injured self, or find water or carefully plan your day, a map beats "word of mouth" any day. And, it provides a detailed, human-checked context for your whereabouts that no consumer-level GPS device or "app" can. Not to mention: no downloading or batteries required. Also, the one with the map is the most popular one in the shelter at night.

Offering the most thorough coverage, the 11 official *Appalachian Trail Guides*—no relation to the thru-hiking book of the same name above—describe all relevant features and detail mileage between landmarks. Packaged in a resealable plastic bag, each pocket-sized guide includes a set of water- and tear-resistant topographic maps. Consider sending the maps to strategic mail drops along the trail.

To purchase guides and maps, visit the Ultimate A.T. Store at <www.atctrailstore.org> or call 1-888-AT-STORE (888-287-8673). The Web sites

Indulgences

Finally, a list of *wants* to add to your *needs*, as space and inclination allow:

Town Clothes

For those who want to feel "human" while in town, consider forwarding a cardboard box full of comfortable clothes, shoes, shaving supplies, and such from mail drop to mail drop.

Camp Shoes

Pack a pair of favorite Teva-type sandals, moccasins, or Crocs/Waldees—they'll feel wonderful after a long day of hiking and still protect your feet from sharp rocks and sticks. They reduce your impact around camp, are easy to slip on when nature calls in the middle of the night, and can serve as "town shoes."

Coffee Supplies

While freeze-dried coffee is terrible, going without is unthinkable to many of us. Here's all you need: a heavy-duty plastic funnel, paper coffee filters, and ground coffee. Place the funnel in your cup and a filter into the funnel, then pour in coffee grounds (experiment to find the right amount) followed by boiling water. Keep everything in a resealable plastic bag.

BakePacker

This 4-ounce aluminum grid (about $15) fits inside a 6- to 7-inch pot, enabling users to bake fresh biscuits or bread over boiling water. It includes a recipe book.

Fun & Games

For rainy days, pack a travel chess set or deck of playing cards. The Ultimate Appalachian Trail Store also has a couple of made-for-the-trail backpacking games. It's up to you to find an opponent.

Monocular/Binoculars

Birders will be especially thankful they packed a monocular or pair of compact binoculars.

Trail Mascot

Some hikers can't help but pack a rubber ducky, Barbie, or other synthetic doo-dad as a trip mascot (suitable as a desk ornament in later years). One hiker even carried a plastic pink flamingo all the way to Katahdin.

of REI, Eastern Mountain Sports (EMS), Barnes & Noble, and Amazon also are good sources for the whole array.

Compass/GPS

The A.T. is generally well-marked and -trafficked. Unless you plan to do some off-trail hiking, a compass isn't required equipment (and the iron ore in the rocks along many sections of the A.T. can fool the inexperienced). Do be careful on switchbacks, though, as you may find out too late that you've left the A.T. to follow a drainage ditch.

Similarly, GPS devices are becoming of some value to thru-hikers, but tree cover and other technical issues can interfere with signal strength. That said, some hikers appreciate the ability to mark favorite spots and check elevation. Make your call based on weight and convenience. Likewise, tracking devices beloved by those worried at home—such as DeLorme's InReach or SPOT—have pros and cons; Outdoor Gear Lab features technical reviews.

Books & Music

These borderline indulgences are a must for bibliophiles and audiophiles. Books pose the biggest problem in terms of pack space and weight. One workaround is to send books ahead by mail drop at readable intervals, but you may be surprised at just how many of today's hikers bring along e-readers, including iPads and other tablets. Some "smartphones" allow many of the options that only a few years ago required separate devices.

On the music front, digital technology has come to the rescue with compact MP3 players, such as Apple's popular iPod, on which you can store up to 10,000 songs (that's 55 songs a day on the trail). Its rechargeable batteries last 12 to 15 hours and allow a two-hour fast charge for hikers in a hurry.

Although not customizable, even-smaller FM radios enable users to catch local weather forecasts, news, and the latest sports scores.

One caveat: Don't play music so loud that you annoy fellow hikers or miss a warning rattle or growl from a trailside animal.

Chapter ☑ Checklist

**Opposite the Gear Checklist is a Food Checklist
(page 83) arranged by meal, as well as lists
of popular snacks, spices, condiments, and drinks.
Use it to develop shopping lists for resupply stops.
Refer to the checklist and the following dietary suggestions,
but, in the end, you're master chef
of your own trail menu.**

The one given regarding food requirements on long-distance hikes is quantity. Hiking is strenuous, and thru-hikers burn an estimated 4,000 to 6,000 calories each day. Dieting is out of the question, as some men (fewer women) lose 10 to 20 percent of their body weight, regardless of how much they eat.

If replacement calories were unavailable, someone hiking a dozen or more miles a day would become a candidate for malnutrition. No matter how tired you are at day's end, make a conscious effort to take in enough food for basic health and strength.

How much is enough? To compensate for 4,000-plus burned calories, plan on consuming about 2 pounds of food per day.

Food can be heavy. At 2 pounds per day, 10 days' worth of food weighs 20 pounds—enough to turn a manageable 40-pound pack into a misery-inducing 60-pound pack. The trick is to carry food that provides plenty of calories but doesn't weigh much. In general, that means carrying food that contains little or no water.

Prepackaged, freeze-dried backpacker meals are ideal. At $4 to $7 a packet, they are too expensive for most thru-hikers to use on a six-month hike, although some outfitters do offer bulk discounts. Decide for yourself whether the cost is worth the convenience.

Food Planner

To move beyond the basics of food planning, pick up a copy of Lou Adsmond's *The Appalachian Trail Food Planner,* which offers detailed planning advice and schedules, clip-out cooking tips, and trail recipes. See appendix (page 56) for more details.

It is more economical to dehydrate one's own food. A basic dehydrator costs between $30 and $60 and often comes with recipes. To dehydrate a meal, you cook at home as usual, put the cooked food in the dehydrator for several hours, then place the dehydrated meal in a resealable plastic bag. Since each meal takes several hours to dehydrate, you'll need to begin this process months in advance of your hike. Be sure to write the preparation date and meal description on each bag. Dehydrated food will keep for the duration of your thru-hike.

Thru-hikers report that food expenses run about $8 to $16 per day per hiker (excluding restaurant visits). Costs vary depending on the types of food one purchases, how it is pre prepared, and the chosen resupply method (town visits or mail drops).

Some hikers have the romantic notion to live off wild foods along the trail. While you'll find such edible plants as ramps, fiddlehead ferns, Solomon's seal, strawberries, blackberries, raspberries, and blueberries, they don't grow in sustainable quantities. It's fine to pick the occasional handful of berries—just know what you're eating. Keep in mind, too, that birds and wild animals have no other options if hikers consume all their wild food sources.

So, what should you include in your diet? According to *The Appalachian Trail Food Planner*, caloric intake should be about 50 percent carbohydrates, 25 percent fats, and 25 percent proteins. Here are some staples:

Fats—The most concentrated source of calories, fats are usually worth their pack weight. Cheese, oil, squeeze margarine, and peanut butter work well, as do cured fatty meats such as pepperoni and summer sausage. If bought during town stops, cheeses and cured meats keep surprisingly well. A longtime hiker favorite is trail mix—high-fat nuts, such as peanuts and sunflower seeds, mixed with dried fruits and chocolate candy.

Starches—Easily dried and rehydrated, starches are popular with thru-hikers because they metabolize quickly, providing needed energy. Dried wheat or corn pastas, grains, cereals, and milled starches such as potatoes and couscous are lightweight and make a good base for meals when combined with water and higher-calorie fats and

Bears & Food

Black bears roam the length of the **A.T.** While they are generally wary of humans, the same doesn't hold true for our food. They will gladly scavenge that half-eaten hot dog or candy bar you left out. Don't let them. Encouraged by treats or chance food, bears lose their fear of people and become nuisances or worse.

Bear-bagging is essential where food-storage systems are not available. A stuff sack and a 50-foot length of rope are all you need to safeguard your food and other "smellables" from local Yogis. First, put your food in the sack, grab your rope, and find a tree well away from camp. Next, throw one end of the rope over a branch at least 18 feet high (on a spot at least 6 feet from the trunk) and tie that end to the sack. Finally, hoist the sack up to 6 feet below the branch and tie the rope's loose end to a rock or another trunk well away from the host tree.

Avoid the lazy hiker's method: hanging food in the shelter. Just because no bears have been reported at that shelter recently doesn't mean you might not be tempting one tonight.

Although bulkier and more expensive than stuff sacks, bear canisters are another option and required if overnighting in a short section in Georgia.

proteins. Many flavored mixes, such as those made by Lipton and Mahatma, are available in grocery stores, or you can make your own in advance. Breads are bulky, and most yeast breads spoil quickly; flatbreads (such as packaged flour tortillas) keep much better, as do crackers and low-moisture homemade "hiker breads," such as Logan bread.

Proteins—Later in a hike, once you've burned off excess body fat and built up muscle, high-protein foods are important to preserve muscle and bone mass. Good candidates include fatty meats such as summer sausages, lean meats such as beef jerky, dried hamburger, dried eggs, and dried vegetable proteins. Foil pouches or small cans of tuna or chicken work as additions to a base, but big cans of soup and stews, which are high in water content, aren't worth the weight. You'll also need to pack out the cans as trash.

Salts—Dried soups, bouillon, and powdered sports-drink mixes are good sources of electrolytes and salts, which you'll sweat out in hot weather.

Sugars—Particularly when the weather is cold and damp, snack on high-sugar foods, such as candy and granola bars, energy bars, and dried fruits to balance your metabolism between meals. Many thru-hikers snack every hour or two to boost energy levels.

Liquids—Hikers should drink a minimum of a gallon of water per day. Treat all water from natural sources (see page 51). Many hikers complain about the taste of water treated with iodine tablets. One solution is to dip a tea bag in the water or add a flavored-drink packet.

Meal Planning

To save pack weight and space, thru-hikers typically repackage most foods they carry, throwing out bulky cardboard, plastic, and polystyrene packages and storing the food in resealable plastic bags. Repackaging can be done in bulk before the hike begins, although some foods, such as dried meats and candy bars, should remain in their original packages to avoid spoilage. If those are purchased near the trail, spoilage is less of an issue.

Stick to average portion sizes for the first week of the hike, particularly if you are overweight, then start increasing your food intake. When pre-measuring portions for mail drops, add more food than you would normally eat at home, particularly for the last couple months of the hike, when you'll be desperate for calories. The trick is to correctly predict your needs. Too much food and your pack weight will slow you down. Sure, you'll eat well, but you'll also burn more calories on steep climbs and descents.

Conversely, hikers carrying too little food may come up short between town visits, although they can always adjust for their needs as the hike progresses. They may pay a bit more for food upfront, but they save on postage, and a lighter pack means a faster pace. Do bear in mind that hours change and businesses close—pack at least a day's worth of food in reserve to anticipate any unexpected changes to your itinerary.

Take Your Vitamins!

Since it's difficult to maintain a well-balanced diet on the trail (fresh fruit and vegetables are hard to keep), add a daily multivitamin to your regimen. Keep vitamins dry in a resealable plastic bag.

The next chapter (pages 43–46) discusses resupply options in detail. While the Mail Drop Locations chart on page 84 lists towns where mail and supplies are readily available, be sure to consult the annual *Appalachian Trail Data Book* and *Appalachian Trail Thru-Hikers' Companion* for thorough, updated information on trail-town services and supplies.

Cooking

While a few minimalists go stoveless, eating only energy bars, trail mix, and various concoctions that don't require heating or cooking, most thru-hikers carry a lightweight stove and fuel. Not only does a stove enable you to prepare better meals, it's also an important safety measure, as hot food can help ward off hypothermia.

Backpacking catalogs are full of neat gadgets for the culinary-minded hiker: espresso makers, corn poppers, ovens, and nested cookware sets. Although you may spot a few of those on the trail, most thru-hikers soon realize all they need is a pot, a lid, and a spoon. The rest is just extra weight.

Dinner preparation is often a simple matter of boiling water, stirring in rehydrated or freeze-dried food, adding spices, oils, and proteins, simmering the meal a few minutes, and waiting until it's cool enough to spoon out of the pot. Few have the energy for anything more involved.

Traditionally, thru-hikers have carried stoves that burn white gas (or Coleman fuel), a naphtha that burns hot, even in cold weather. White gas is more readily available along the trail than the sealed butane and propane cartridges popular with weekend hikers. Recent years have also seen an upswing in the use of can stoves (page 31), lightweight alcohol-burning stoves made from discarded aluminum cans. Other lightweight options include fuel tablets and wood-burning stoves.

It is possible to develop elaborate recipes for lightweight stoves, and each year a few intrepid thru-hikers manage a gourmet hike. But, if you're like most thru-hikers, you'll want meals that are simple and cheap, don't take long to fix, and provide lots of calories. That said, variety is important on a long thru-hike, so take advantage of trail-town laundry stops to forage on salads and greens and pick up a treat or two.

Put a Lid on It!

Always use a lid when cooking— particularly when boiling water. The lid will shorten cooking times, keep food warm, and save precious fuel. An aluminum windscreen shortens your cooking time, even on still days, and is essential on windy days.

Chapter ☑ Worksheet

**Now that you have a rough idea of your itinerary,
as well as what gear and food you'll need on your thru-hike,
think about how many mail drops you might send.
Rip out the Mail Drop Locations chart (page 84) and compare
it to your existing itinerary. Using the Sample Resupply Itinerary (page 90)
as a guide, draft your own Resupply Itinerary (page 92).
Once you've finalized your plans and assembled your packages,
keep the forms handy in your backpack.**

No matter how strong you are, you won't be able to carry the requisite ton of food, water, and gear to sustain you on your thru-hike. As pack animals aren't allowed on the trail, that leaves resupply as your only option.

While the A.T. does enter the backcountry, it's a far cry from the untrammeled wilderness one finds in parts of Alaska, Canada, and the western United States. This narrow corridor of protected land threads through the nation's most densely populated states. You'll regularly approach small towns where you can pick up parcels, purchase supplies, and/or meet loved ones delivering care packages. It's almost never necessary to carry anything more than a week's worth of food. There's only one remote stretch, in northern Maine, where thru-hikers may have to carry eight to 10 days' worth of supplies, but even that can be broken into smaller segments.

Thru-hikers typically employ two main resupply strategies:

1. Resupply along the trail.

2. Resupply with mail drops.

Mail drops are the traditional choice but today the one far less pursued. Using this method, a thru-hiker prepares boxes at home

Trail Yellow Pages

The annual *Appalachian Trail Thru-Hikers' Companion* and comparable guides feature detailed notes on lodgings, stores, restaurants, and other services along the trail, including directions and contact information. Buy or borrow a copy, and use it in conjunction with this planner to determine your resupply schedule. See appendix (page 56) for details.

filled with food and gear and asks a family member or friend to ship the packages to post offices or businesses along the route at regular intervals. Out on the trail, the hiker walks/hitchhikes to each mail drop, picks up the supplies, repacks, and keeps hiking.

As trail-town services have improved, many thru-hikers have chosen to simply resupply along the way. In fact, it is possible to forgo mail drops altogether, although many hikers combine approaches—supplementing regular mail drops with purchases at local stores.

Mail Drops

As strange as it may seem, you don't have to live in a town to receive mail there. Imagine you're running short on supplies. Prior to your scheduled arrival in, say, Monson, Maine, someone can send a package in your name to the address *General Delivery, Monson, ME 04464.* All you have to do is stop by Monson's post office, show a photo ID, and request your mail.

Thru-hikers have long used mail drops to resupply. In recent years, numerous trail-town hostels, motels, hiking outfitters, and other services also have agreed to hold packages for thru-hikers. In fact, hikers prefer the latter to post offices, as they remain open after hours and on weekends and will accept packages from UPS, Federal Express, and other shippers. (Post offices accept only U.S. mail, and a number of A.T.-related post offices have shown up on recent lists of ones to be closed to help reduce USPS deficits. To add to the confusion, UPS and FedEx these days contract with some post offices to deliver their packages the final leg.)

Mail drops reduce one's upfront costs, as you can purchase nonperishable food in bulk and prepare it in advance—particularly handy for hard-to-find items or such menu staples as pastas, grains and beans, powders, and bulky canned items. Mail drops are also useful for meeting such foreseeable needs as replacement socks, summer clothes, batteries, candles, journals, books, and maps.

The big disadvantage of mail drops is that they lock you in to choices before you really know what life on the trail is all about. Suppose you buy a summer's worth of mac and cheese, but get sick of it after the first month? And, although buying in bulk is cheaper upfront, postage costs mount up quickly. In an ATC

Three Ways to Send Mail Drops

1. To a post office, first class.

2. To a post office, parcel post insured (cheaper, but takes longer).

Address package:
    Your Name
    General Delivery
    Town, State ZIP Code

3. To a hostel, motel, or other place, by Postal Service, FedEx, or UPS.

Address package:
    Your Name
    Name & Phone # of Lodging
    Full Street Address
    Town, State ZIP Code

Do *not* include the words "General Delivery" on a package sent to any location other than a post office: It will never leave the post office.

On *all* packages, write off to the side, "Hold for northbound (or southbound) A.T. hiker," with an ETA. Be sure to include a return address.

survey, nearly a quarter of successful thru-hikers said they wouldn't use mail drops on a repeat hike.

As it is, most thru-hikers send fewer than 20 mail drops. Be ruthless when choosing items, repackage everything in resealable plastic bags, and leave boxes unsealed until mailing, so supplies can be removed or added as necessary. When choosing mail-drop locations, stick to towns either close to the trail or those with other attractions — long mail-drop detours are tiresome.

For emergency shipments of equipment or money, consult your *Companion* for the nearest post office (in bold in the text and tables, including the ZIP

Getting to Town

Although a few towns straddle the trail, most are several miles away — miles a footsore thru-hiker would just as soon avoid. It may seem easier just to carry more stuff, until you cross several mountains with an overweight pack. One option is to thumb a ride.

Trail-town residents have learned over the years that, while hikers may be a bit "aromatic," they're mostly friendly folks who boost the local economy. Hikers, in turn, have seen beyond stereotypes and met the mostly good-hearted folk of rural eastern Appalachia. That said, hitchhiking does carry inherent risks. To avoid any mishaps, avoid hitching alone, and don't accept a ride from anyone who makes you uncomfortable. Hitchhiking is prohibited on interstate highways, some state highways, the Blue Ridge Parkway, and Skyline Drive in Shenandoah National Park.

Another option is to arrange a hiker shuttle. Arrangements are best made at least a week or two in advance. A list of known providers is available for download on the Appalachian Trail Conservancy Web site (www.appalachiantrail.org) or on request by mail or telephone from ATC: Appalachian Trail Conservancy, Attn: Shuttle List, P.O. Box 807, Harpers Ferry, WV 25425; (304) 535-6331.

Thru-hikers vary in the amount of time they choose to spend off-trail. Hit-and-run hikers make day trips to town, saving both time and money. Such hikers camp within a hour or two of a road crossing, hitch into town in the morning, resupply, do laundry, eat lunch at a local restaurant, then hitch back to the trail in the afternoon.

Other hikers stay overnight. Arriving in town in the afternoon, they stop by the post office, find a room for the night, eat dinner, clean up, do laundry, shop, and/or socialize with other hikers. Most hitch out the following morning, while others stay on to recuperate. Just remember: The more time you spend in town, the more money you'll spend and the longer you'll take to finish.

Code and distance from the trail).

Resupply along the Trail

Rarely will you find yourself more than a few days from a road crossing that presents an easy hitch to trail-town supermarkets, convenience stores, and restaurants. A growing number of towns now host hiking outfitters, where you can buy replacement gear. Sometimes it's nice just to get off the trail and recuperate, hobnob with locals, and enjoy a satisfying sit-down meal.

Resupplying on the go has many advantages. Obviously, it's the only way to purchase such perishable items as fresh fruit and vegetables, baked goods, and that all-important hiker staple, ice cream. You also don't have to be as prescient about forecasting your needs and changing tastes—you're free to purchase a variety of foods, experiment with new gear, and incorporate suggestions from fellow hikers.

On the downside, you'll pay more for supplies in small-town groceries, convenience marts, and camp stores, although brand-name supermarkets have expanded their reach. Your selections may be limited, though, and you'll be tempted to pick up impulse items.

The Best of Both

For the best outcome, blend aspects of each approach. Buy a variety of staples from a local warehouse club or food co-op, mixing in a goody or two, and arrange a mail drop every other week. On alternate weeks, buy what you need from local stores, including fresh produce and indulgences. Consider splitting bulk purchases with fellow hikers.

Another favorite among thru-hikers is a bounce box—a package you forward from town to town, "bouncing" it north or south ahead of you. For instance, you might buy bulk groceries and supplies in one town, stow a week's worth in your backpack, and mail the rest to a town 100 miles farther north. Or, if you're toting a bulky winter sweater and the weather warms up, you can forward it to a mail drop in a cooler climate.

Many-times thru-hiker "Baltimore Jack" Tarlin offers his perspectives on this subject in an excellent article, "AT Resupply Info," a link to which can be found on the home page of <www.whiteblaze.net>.

Chapter ☑ Worksheet

**Fill out the Emergency Medical Information
worksheet on page 93.
Carry this form with you on the trail,
and be sure to leave a copy
with a family member or friend.**

The beginning of a thru-hike is a wake-up call for most hikers—the moment of truth. Your first day of hiking offers a taste of what the entire 2,189-plus miles will be like. In a word: *tough*. Northbound hikers start in Georgia atop Springer Mountain, while southbound hikers begin in Maine by climbing 5,268-foot Katahdin, the state's highest point. Getting to either starting point is a shock to the uninitiated.

Now, the good news: As you become physically conditioned, you'll find such rugged terrain merely challenging, rather than tortuous. Within a month or two, you'll actually enjoy the exertion and steadily boost your daily mileage. In peak form, you'll be ready for anything the trail can dish out (which is plenty). If you have trouble with insomnia, chances are it will disappear. Fatigue comes quickly after dinner on the trail, and shelter conversation usually ends when the sun sets.

For the first week or two, limit yourself to around 6 to 10 miles per day. Yes, you'll need to average 12 to 15 miles per day over your six-month hike to reach Katahdin (or Springer) before winter, but don't worry about that to begin with. Focus instead on listening to your body. Are you tired 100 feet up the side of a steep mountain, knob, or hill? Rest a while. Do you need to rest

Health Insurance

As you plan your thru-hike, include provisions for medical coverage, in the event you're injured or fall ill. It's usually possible to purchase short-term health insurance. Be sure the policy covers hiking-related injuries and evacuation costs.

Health & Safety

every couple of steps on a steep trail incline? Do it. The point is, don't push yourself too hard early in the hike—you'll be less likely to suffer muscle strains and other injuries. Plan short hiking days and build in plenty of time to sightsee and rest.

Several days or so into your hike, you may find yourself feeling weaker instead of stronger. That probably means your metabolism has accelerated, but your appetite hasn't caught up, and you're running a calorie deficit. You may just need to eat more. It may seem counterintuitive to increase your caloric intake rather than decrease it, but that's exactly what you'll need to do.

After you've been out a couple of weeks, start adding a mile a day to your distance to build stamina. In time, your body will harden, your lungs will clear, your weight will drop (men particularly), and your energy will increase. Just start slowly, gradually build your pace, and then maintain it—you'll succeed.

Fitness

Preparing for the physical and mental challenges of a thru-hike is as much a part of good advance planning as setting your itinerary. While it's possible to complete a thru-hike after starting in poor condition, the trail is difficult enough when you're fit—why give yourself an additional handicap? At the very least, begin a moderate exercise program several months before departure, so you aren't overwhelmed at the outset.

If you're overweight, try to lose a few pounds before you hike. Don't eat less; exercise more—you'll need your strength. Older people and those who have led sedentary lives should consult a doctor first. The more pre-existing health issues you have, the more information and guidance you'll need to get into shape before you start.

Thru-hikers tone up using a range of common exercises, including walking, running, swimming, aerobics, calisthenics, cross-country skiing, weightlifting, biking, even climbing stairs. Of course, hiking itself offers a challenging and relevant fitness regimen. Get out on as many day hikes and camping trips as possible to places that approximate the trail's rolling terrain. Prehike weight training helps strengthen muscles and tendons for the grind, but nothing beats hiking steep grades with a pack on your back. Build up slowly to your full pack weight, and be sure to wear the boots and gear you'll be taking on your thru-hike. Don't let bad weather stop you—rain certainly won't let up when you're out on the trail.

When you do hit the trail, remember to give your body time to adjust to the stresses of daily exercise, stretch once muscles are warm, and help it wind down by stretching as you ready your campsite. Don't push your body too hard—it may push back with shin splints, tendonitis, or worse. Because hiking isn't an upper-body exercise, you may lose muscle mass in your chest and arms. Trekking poles may help prevent this, as well as ease the stress on knees.

Finally, ignore any real or perceived pressure from your partner or group.

I Can Quit Anytime I Want

No more excuses—the lead-up to a thru-hike is the perfect time to quit smoking. If nothing else, you'll appreciate your renewed lung power and energy on those steep, higher-elevation climbs!

Mental Fitness

Psychological problems loom as large as physical difficulties for hikers. They take several forms and are less obvious. Depending on your age and finances, an A.T. thru-hike can affect your career, family relationships, friendships, and retirement plans. Disconnected from everyday life, hikers are thrown into a rambling, day-to-day existence, one of both high highs and intense lows.

Natural phenomena such as heat waves and prolonged rains drive many hikers off the trail. But then, Mother Nature ain't your mama.

Humans' inherent competitiveness also takes its toll. Some drop out in defeat after being left in the dust one too many times, while others bemoan the mile-bagging mentality of *überhikers* they thought they'd left behind in "civilization."

Others miss that civilization—TV, double lattés, the latest movie releases, regular showers. With every blister, thunderstorm, and smelly morning, they question their commitment until the drive to go home supersedes their desire to finish what they started.

Another challenge is the inevitable drop-off among fellow hikers. If you lose your hiking partner, this can be particularly discouraging.

Many simply grow lonely or bored, subject to recurring bouts of depression. Thru-hikers often call this the "Virginia Blues," as Virginia's 552 trail miles (counting those atop the West Virginia line for two day-long jaunts) represent the longest single stretch—a quarter of the over-all trail.

So, what's the key to overcoming the mind games and reaching trail's end? A positive attitude. Be aware of the mental challenges that lie ahead, and develop strategies to deal with them as they arise. If someone passes you, just smile, say hello, and maintain your pace. If a partner drops out, wish him/her well and resolve to see it through for both of you. Do you miss the creature comforts? Stop in town a few days and get your fix—the trail will wait.

Trail Hazards

Thru-hiking is strenuous activity that will subject your body to a vigorous workout virtually every day for several months. It's important to take care of yourself throughout the hike, particularly during the first several weeks, as your body adjusts. At the end of every hiking day, take aspirin, ibuprofen (Advil), or acetaminophen (Tylenol) to ward off pain and swelling and help you rest. Treat other symptoms as they arise.

While wildlife along the A.T. is relatively benign in comparison to some western species, you should learn to recognize and avoid a few critters. A few are listed on page 53.

Following is a list of common health concerns and basic advice.

Blisters

As you hike, your feet will toughen, and large, thick calluses will develop at strategic points on the soles of your feet. Before you get calluses, you'll have to protect your feet from blisters, which can make hiking or even walking agony. An infected blister can even become a serious health threat.

Blister prevention is the key to avoiding problems. Wearing two pairs of synthetic hiking socks should help (see page 26).

In your first-aid kit, carry such products as Spenco 2nd Skin, Band-Aid Advanced Healing strips and Liquid Bandage, molefoam, and moleskin. When a blister forms, first use a sterile pin/needle to relieve the pressure, then use antibiotic ointment. Next, apply Spenco 2nd Skin or Liquid Bandage to the surface, and cover the blister with moleskin or molefoam. This combination should ease pressure and allow the skin to heal.

Chafing

Chafing often occurs in wet weather, when damp fabrics rub repeatedly against the skin. To avoid this, wear loose-fitting synthetic clothes and stay away from cotton. Rinse clothes after hiking to remove body salts. To treat chafed skin, apply talcum powder or a rash ointment.

Stress Fractures

Stress fractures are hairline cracks in the bones of the feet, often caused by continual excessive impact. Thru-hikers are particularly vulnerable early in their trek, before leg and foot muscles grow strong enough to take the stress off bones. Carrying an overweight pack and pushing oneself too hard are primary causes of stress fractures.

Sole Solace

Many thru-hikers follow a nightly ritual to put their feet into a state of bliss. After removing boots and socks and rinsing your feet, first apply rubbing alcohol with a bandanna, then sprinkle foot powder on your tired tootsies. A few minutes of deep rubbing, and you'll feel like you just may make it to Maine after all. Store the rubbing alcohol and foot powder in small containers and keep them in a resealable plastic bag.

Carry a reasonable load, start slow, and tread gently. Avoid stomping or running downhill.

Like any broken bone, a stress fracture is a serious matter and typically gets worse if ignored. The only treatment is to stop hiking, see a doctor, and wait for it to heal.

Gastrointestinal Illness

The causes of diarrhea and intestinal discomfort can range from drinking untreated water to food poisoning to slow adjustment to life (and food) on the trail. If diarrhea lasts more than a couple of days, however, it's time to find a doctor. You won't be able to "tough it out" if it's the waterborne protozoan *Giardia lamblia*, which keeps getting worse until treated with antibiotics. Untreated, it can lead to dehydration and weakness. Please report any outbreaks of "stomach bugs" to local health departments and ATC (at <www.appalachiantrail.org/stomachbug>).

When out on the trail, avoid drinking from questionable water sources and treat all water with filters, purifiers, or chemicals or by boiling it for several minutes. *Maintain proper personal hygiene, washing your hands before all meals and especially after defecating.* In recent years, many hikers have been waylaid by some type of surface-borne, norovirus-type illness. Share gorp food with other hikers in ways that don't allow transmission of germs; don't pass around a bag and let others dip in hands that might not be as clean as yours; wash raw fruits thoroughly. Bury all human waste in a 6- to 8-inch deep "cathole" at least 200 feet from any water source, camp, or trail.

Dehydration

Dehydration sets in when the body's water output (through excessive sweating) exceeds one's water intake. The deficiency can lead to decreased electrolytes and a dangerous rise in blood-sodium levels. Warning signs include decreased sweating, nausea, dizziness, and confusion. Severe dehydration can lead to a coma, organ damage, and death.

Thru-hikers should drink a minimum of one gallon of water per day. Consider purchasing an integrated hydration system for your backpack (see page 32). If you do feel any of the symptoms described above, replace both water and salt levels, either by consuming a sports drink high in electrolytes or eating a salty snack when you stop for water.

Heat Exhaustion & Heat Stroke

Prolonged exposure to heat can pose a true threat during summer months, particularly if you're hiking alone. While heat exhaustion is debilitating, heat stroke can be deadly. Symptoms of heat exhaustion include drenching sweat, clammy skin, and faintness. If it progresses to heat stroke, the body temperature soars, the heart rate may double, and a person may suffer convulsions and lose consciousness.

When temperatures soar, increase your water intake, and scale back your hiking pace. Do most of your hiking in the cooler morning and evening

Health & Safety

hours and consider taking a midday siesta between 10 a.m. and 2 p.m., the hottest part of the day. If you encounter someone with heatstroke symptoms, place them in the shade, immerse them in water or cool them with wet clothing, and seek immediate medical aid.

Sunburn

On the A.T., sunburn is more of a risk in early spring and late fall, when trees are bare. It's also a concern along stretches above the treeline in New Hampshire's White Mountains. To avoid it, wear a wide-brimmed hat and cover exposed skin with sunscreen (minimum SPF 15). Don't overlook such precautions in the excitement of starting your thru-hike.

Hypothermia

Among the most serious health threats thru-hikers face, hypothermia is a dangerously low body temperature that often follows prolonged exposure to cold, wet, windy conditions. Well beyond a simple chill, the rapid heat loss slows reaction times and impairs judgment. You can die. Because it affects brain function, hypothermia victims often can't recognize the symptoms themselves, so it's important to monitor your fellow hikers. Shivering and confusion are early signs.

Be prepared for cold, wet conditions along the trail for much of the spring and fall. Hypothermia can occur even in light rain and temperatures in the low 50s. Wear layered synthetic clothing with a waterproof shell and avoid cotton. While hiking itself will raise your body temperature, the danger lies in getting chilled while stopped. At the end of each day, find shelter quickly, change into dry clothing, consume hot food and liquids, and slip into a warm, dry sleeping bag to restore body heat.

Frostbite

Usually only a concern in winter months, frostbite is a condition in which one's flesh actually freezes, causing permanent damage. Exposed hands and feet are most vulnerable, so be sure to protect them with adequate gloves and footwear. If you suspect frostbite, slowly warm the affected area in tolerably hot water, cover it in clean bandages, and seek medical attention. Do not place the victim before a fire or rub frostbitten skin with snow.

Allergies & Poison Ivy

Before leaving on a thru-hike, assess your susceptibility to allergic reactions from bee stings, pollen, poison ivy, and anything else found in nature that could pose a threat. If you're prone to severe allergic reactions, talk to your doctor.

If you suspect contact with poison ivy, wash your skin with a strong cleanser, such as Tecnu or Zanfel. Place contaminated clothing in a separate plastic garbage bag and launder it as soon as possible. Treat any resulting rash with cortisone cream and calamine lotion. Severe breakouts may require medical attention.

Insect Bites & Lyme Disease

Thru-hikers contend with no-see-ums, horse and deer flies, blackflies, and mosquitoes for the length of the trail. Insect repellent with DEET (see page 35) is the most effective defense, while a tent with no-see-um netting should enable pest-free sleeping.

Ticks are a *much more serious* concern, however, because they are carriers of Lyme disease or, more rarely and more recently, BMD (*borrelia miyamotoi* disease), both of which can cause fever, chills, and joint pain and lead to long-term chronic problems if not promptly treated with antibiotics. Many thru-hikers succumb to this infection, and your exposure increases significantly once you reach (northbound) northern Virginia or (southbound) New Hampshire. Early Lyme symptoms include a red spot at the bite point that often (about 60 to 70 percent of the time) expands within days into a six-inch bull's-eye mark. If you suspect infection, promptly see a doctor. *These threats should not be viewed casually.*

Applied to clothing, permethrin will kill ticks on contact. Regularly check your skin for ticks. Use tweezers to remove any you find. Try not to squeeze the body; pinch the head, and draw it slowly out of the skin.

Mice

Permanent residents at many shelters, mice bear fleas and ticks and may carry diseases. Secure all food and scented items in a stuff sack. Avoid using "mouse baffles" (upside-down cans hung from string) in shelters. They may deter mice but won't deter bears and other critters.

Snakes

Poisonous (rattlesnakes, copperheads) and nonpoisonous snakes are common along the trail, particularly in warm weather, although most are typically passive and seldom seen. Watch where you step and where you place your hands in rough sections. If someone is bitten, clean the wound, keep the victim as still and calm as possible, and seek medical attention. Consider including a snakebite kit in your first-aid supplies.

Avoid killing snakes. Some are protected under the Endangered Species Act.

Bears

Black bears (no grizzlies!) live along much of the A.T. Most are wary of humans, although they can be pretty persistent when in search of food. If a bear does approach, slowly back away. If one attacks, fight back aggressively—do not run away or play dead.

To discourage bears, store all food and scented objects (powders, chewing gum) in a stuff sack, and hang it from a tree branch well away from camp or the shelter. This practice is referred to as bear-bagging (see page 40).

First Aid

Most thru-hikers find a comprehensive first-aid kit too heavy to carry, but you should carry a basic kit that can treat scrapes, blisters, and aches. Remember to carry any prescription medication, including refill forms. Also learn something about first aid ahead of time. Consider enrolling in a first-aid training course through the Red Cross or your local YMCA.

The sidebar at left lists basic first-aid supplies you should carry on your thru-hike. Keep the items clean and dry in resealable plastic bags. Consult a doctor before using any medication in large doses.

Personal Safety

Crime rates are low along the A.T., and common sense should keep you out of most fixes.

Before leaving home, provide copies of your itinerary and any emergency medical information to a trusted relative or friend. (On the other hand, do not post your location or itinerary in real time on on-line journals.) On the trail, be sure to sign all available shelter registers with your trail name and surname. When a hiker goes missing, authorities often check these registers first.

Try to avoid hiking alone. If you are solo, stick to well-trodden paths. Network with couples and groups that are keeping pace with you—thru-hikers typically watch out for one another. When meeting strangers, size them up and present a confident manner. If someone does act suspicious, be courteous and move on. Report any threatening encounters to authorities (try 9-1-1 first) as soon as possible, and mention such incidents in shelter registers.

If you arrive at a shelter and are uneasy about your potential companions, announce plans to hike on, then pitch your tent safely off the trail. Don't camp near roads.

Although it's a common practice among thru-hikers, avoid hitchhiking alone whenever possible. Again, size up the driver, and decide for yourself whether it's an acceptable risk. While in town, keep an eye on your belongings, and be aware of your surroundings.

For safety, carry both a whistle and a flashlight. The common distress signal is either three short blasts on the whistle or three short flashes from your light. Aside from the weight and other shortcomings, to carry a firearm on the trail you must meet a whole series of federal and state requirements (and it's only legal in states that allow carrying in their own state parks).

Check ATC's Web site (www.appalachiantrail.org) for more detailed tips, as well as information about local hunting seasons. In seasons, remain on the trail and wear blaze orange for visibility.

Should you surf a few Web sites and pick up other books and maps to plan your thru-hike? Absolutely. At least borrow a few books during the planning stages, whether or not you carry them in your pack. Refer to maps for elevation profiles and a sense of terrain, so you can plan a realistic daily pace rather than the trip-long average.

As a compact reference, the *Appalachian Trail Data Book* offers up-to-date (as of each December) information about distances and facilities. Also recommended are ATC's official trail maps, which show most springs, creeks, and campsites. Other books, such as ALDHA's *Appalachian Trail Thru-Hikers' Companion*, published by ATC, or the self-published *Appalachian Trail Guide* by David "AWOL" Miller, offer detailed information about trail-town services and supplies.

Dozens of useful Web sites and Facebook pages are available to help you plan your thru-hike and even make the most relevant use of electronic gadgets. Join a hiker forum to read first-hand trail experiences, browse honest gear appraisals, and line up potential hiking partners. Visit sites devoted to gearheads and lightweight hikers for a different take on thru-hike equipment needs.

Recommended Reading

The following is a partial list of popular books related to thru-hiking and the Appalachian Trail. In addition to the books listed below, the Appalachian Trail Conservancy (ATC) publishes and/or distributes the 11 official

Appendix

Appalachian Trail Guides that cover the length of the trail and are updated every four to five years, with changes in between reported in the *Data Book*. Each guide is packaged in a resealable plastic bag and includes a set of water- and tear-resistant topographic maps of the sections covered in the guidebook. Hikers' memoirs are another potent source of tips.

For a thorough list and to purchase books and maps, visit the Ultimate A.T. Store online at www.atctrailstore.org or call (888) AT STORE (888-287-8673) to place an order or have a catalogue mailed to you.

Appalachian Trail

Appalachian Trail Data Book, by Daniel D. Chazin. Harpers Ferry, W.Va.: Appalachian Trail Conservancy (annual).

Appalachian Trail Thru-Hikers' Companion, by the Appalachian Long Distance Hikers Association. Harpers Ferry, W.Va.: Appalachian Trail Conservancy (annual).

Appalachian Trail Book of Profiles, Appalachian Trail Conservancy, 2014. *Sample page below left.*

The Appalachian Trail Hiker, by Frank and Victoria Logue. Birmingham, Ala.: Menasha Ridge Press, 2004.

The A.T. Guide: A Handbook for Hiking the Appalachian Trail, by David Miller. Titusville, Fla.: Jerelyn Press (annual).

Appalachian Trials, by Zach Davis. Good Badger Publishing, 2012.

Food

The Appalachian Trail Food Planner, by Lou Adsmond. Harpers Ferry, W.Va.: Appalachian Trail Conservancy, 2012.

Gear

The Ultimate Hiker's Gear Guide: Tools and Techniques to Hit the Trail, by Andrew Skurka. Washington, D.C.: National Geographic Books, 2012.

Lightweight Hiking

Trail Life: Ray Jardine's Lightweight Backpacking, by Ray Jardine. Arizona City, Ariz.: AdventureLore Press, 2012.

Women

Women & Thru-Hiking on the Appalachian Trail, by Beverly "Maine Rose" Hugo. Harpers Ferry, W.Va: Appalachian Trail Conservancy, 2002.

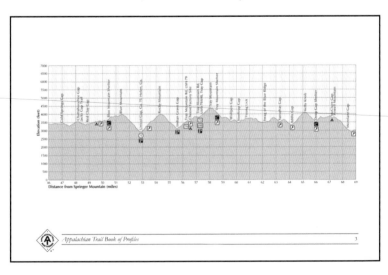

Helpful Web Sites

The ATC Web site, listed first below, includes a roster of trail clubs by state/region. Many of those clubs, primary maintainers of the trail, organize group hikes, sponsor volunteer efforts, and otherwise bring hikers together. Follow the links under the *Who We Are* and *Our Team* links from the home page. Don't forget to search Facebook, YouTube, and even Reddit for A.T. help.

Appalachian Trail

www.appalachiantrail.org
Appalachian Trail Conservancy

www.nps.gov/appa
National Park Service A.T. Park Office

A.T. Hiker Networks

www.aldha.org
Appalachian Long Distance Hikers Association

www.whiteblaze.net
www.appalachiantrials.com
www.appalachiantrailcafe.net
Online communities of A.T. enthusiasts; articles, tables, polls, blogs, photos, fun. Facebook also has a number of thru-hiking forums.

www.backcountry.net
Appalachian Trail List (AT-L)

www.trailjournals.com
Trail journals and thru-hiker network

www.atdist.com
Distance calculator

www.atweather.org
Weather information for trail landmarks

Gear

www.gearfinder.com
Backpacker gear pages

www.backpackgeartest.org
Gear testing and reviews

Hiking & Backpacking

www.backpacker.com
Backpacker magazine on line

www.gorp.com
Great Outdoor Recreation Pages

www.hikingandbackpacking.com
General hiking/backpacking information

Appendix

Topographic Maps

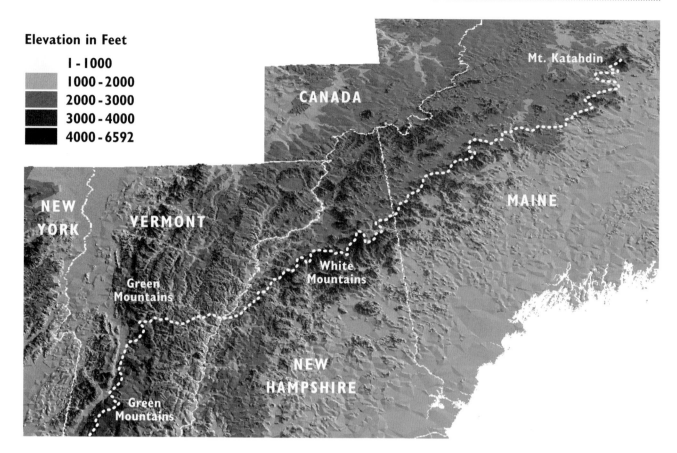

Elevation in Feet

- 1 - 1000
- 1000 - 2000
- 2000 - 3000
- 3000 - 4000
- 4000 - 6592

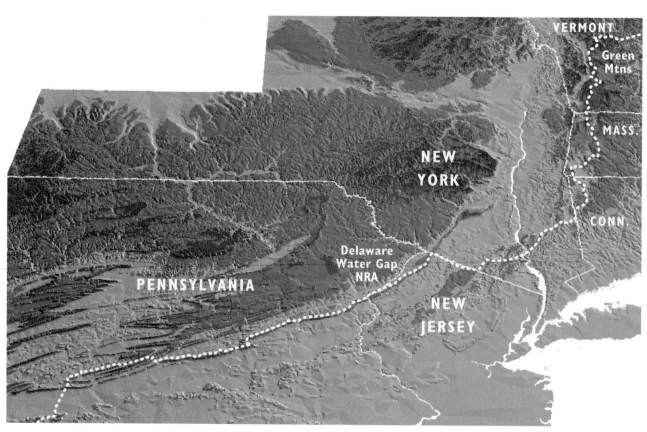

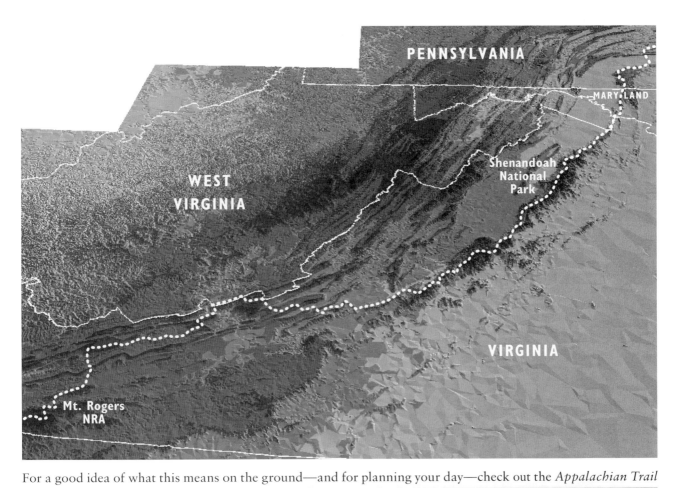

For a good idea of what this means on the ground—and for planning your day—check out the *Appalachian Trail Book of Profiles* (see page 56)

Map List

Following is a list of A.T. maps in north-south order. To purchase maps, visit the Ultimate A.T. Store (www.atctrailstore.org) or call (888) AT STORE.

ATC ITEM NO.	MAPS	TERMINI
101	Maine Map 1	Katahdin to Nahmakanta Lake
Seven maps for Maine sold only as set with guidebook	Maine Map 2	Nahmakanta Lake to West Branch, Pleasant River
	Maine Map 3	West Branch, Pleasant River to Monson
	Maine Map 4	Monson to Kennebec River
	Maine Map 5	Kennebec River to Maine 27
	Maine Map 6	Maine 27 to Maine 17
	Maine Map 7	Maine 17 to Maine/N.H. Line
118	N.H.–Vt. Maps 1 & 2	Maine 26 to U.S. 302 (N.H.)
	N.H.–Vt. Maps 3 & 4	U.S. 302 to Lyme–Dorchester Road (Dartmouth Skiway)
	N.H.–Vt. Maps 5 & 6	Lyme–Dorchester Road (Dartmouth Skiway) to Vt. 140
	N.H.–Vt. Maps 7 & 8	Vt. 140 to Mass. 2 (North Adams)
119	Mass.–Conn. Maps 1 & 2	Vt./Mass Line to Jug End (Mass.)
	Mass.–Conn. Maps 3 & 4	Warner Mtn. (Mass.) to Mt. Egbert (N.Y. Sec. 4)
120	N.Y.–N.J. Maps 1 & 2	N.Y/Conn. Line to N.Y. 17A
	N.Y.–N.J. Maps 3 & 4	N.Y. 17A to N.J./Pa. Line (Delaware Water Gap)
121	Set of five Pennsylvania maps, below	
121A	Keystone Trails Association (KTA) 1–6	Delaware Water Gap to I-81 (Swatara Gap)
121B	KTA 7–8	I-81 to Susquehanna River (Duncannon)
121C	Potomac Appalachian Trail Club (PATC) 1	Susquehanna River to Pa. 94
121D	PATC 2–3	Pa. 94 to U.S. 30
121E	PATC 4	U.S. 30 to Maryland Line
122	PATC 5–6	Maryland
123	PATC 7	Harpers Ferry, W.Va. (Potomac River) to Va. 7
124	PATC 8	Va. 7 to U.S. 522 (Front Royal)
125	PATC 9	U.S. 522 to U.S. 211 (Shenandoah National Park, North District)
126	PATC 10	U.S. 211 to U.S. 33 (Shenandoah National Park, Central District)
127	PATC 11	U.S. 33 to I-64/U.S. 250 (Shen. National Park, South District)
129N	Central Virginia Maps 1 & 2	Rockfish Gap (I-64) to Bearwallow Gap (Blue Ridge Parkway)
	Central Virginia Maps 3 & 4	Bearwallow Gap (Blue Ridge Parkway) to New River (Pearisburg)
131N	Southwest Virginia Maps 1 & 2	New River (Pearisburg) to Rich Valley (Va. 610)
	Southwest Virginia Maps 3 & 4	Poor Valley to Virginia/Tennessee Line
133	Tenn.–N.C Maps 1 & 2	Virginia/Tennessee Line to Indian Grave Gap (Tenn. 395)
	Tenn.–N.C Maps 3 & 4	Indian Grave Gap to I-40 at Great Smoky Mountains National Park
134	National Geographic Map 229	Great Smoky Mountains National Park
135	N.C.–Georgia Maps 1 & 2	Fontana Lake to N.C./Ga. Line (Bly Gap)
	N.C.–Georgia Maps 3 & 4	N.C./Ga. Line to Amicalola Falls State Park, Ga., with approaches

Test Your Trail Savvy

Before you dive into the business of planning your A.T. thru-hike, take the following self-test. Most people who have hiked the whole A.T. will be able to answer these questions. Aspiring thru-hikers would do well to learn the answers before they start. (Answers are at the bottom of page 62.)

▶ TRUE-FALSE

1.	Regulations governing the A.T. can vary in different areas.	T	F
2.	White gas and Coleman fuel are the same thing.	T	F
3.	Thru-hikers have priority at A.T. shelters.	T	F
4.	A.T. thru-hikers must pay a registration fee.	T	F
5.	A good backpack is your most crucial piece of equipment.	T	F
6.	All official A.T. shelters have privies.	T	F
7.	You must average about 12 miles per day to finish the A.T. in six months (180 days).	T	F
8.	You should not start out on the A.T. unless you're carrying two weeks of supplies.	T	F
9.	You'll need a thick, down-filled parka for cold-weather hiking.	T	F
10.	You can count on gentle, springlike weather conditions along the A.T. in Georgia in April.	T	F

▶ MULTIPLE CHOICE

11. Your pack should weigh no more than:
    a. 25 pounds
    b. 35 pounds
    c. 50 pounds
    d. 1/3 your body weight

12. The typical cost of a thru-hike is:
    a. About 25¢ per mile
    b. About what you'd expect to pay to rent a modest apartment
    c. About 50¢ per mile
    d. $4,000 to $6,000

13. A thru-hike is recognized irrespective of:
    a. Pack weight
    b. Direction
    c. Speed
    d. All of the above

14. You are most likely to encounter crowds on the A.T. at the following times and places:
    a. In Georgia during spring-break season
    b. In Great Smoky Mountains National Park in late April and May
    c. In the White Mountains of New Hampshire during late August
    d. All of the above

15. Black bears inhabit:
    a. Only areas known as "bear country"
    b. Only national parks
    c. Only wilderness areas
    d. All parts of the A.T.

16. The worst insects on the trail are:
    a. Blackflies in northern New England in late spring/early summer
    b. Ticks from Virginia to Vermont in late spring and summer
    c. Mosquitoes in Connecticut and Massachusetts in late summer
    d. All of the above

17. The most common danger(s) a thru-hiker typically faces is:
    a. Lightning
    b. Bears and poisonous snakes
    c. Hypothermia and heatstroke
    d. Injury from falling

18. Most thru-hikers resupply themselves by
    a. Mailing themselves food and equipment
    b. Buying food and equipment as they go
    c. Both a & b
    d. Neither a nor b

19. The best way to carry food that won't spoil is:
    a. Carrying canned food
    b. Carrying dried/dehydrated food
    c. Buying fresh supplies along the trail each day
    d. None of the above

20. The most practical clothes are:
    a. Layers of synthetic clothes
    b. Layers of cotton clothes
    c. Layers of woolen clothes
    d. Goose-down clothes

Trail Terms

Following is a selective glossary of key A.T. hiking terms. Hiker jargon is noted in *italics*.

2,000-miler—a thru-hiker or section-hiker who completes the A.T.

A.T.—Appalachian Trail

banana flip—a fall in which your feet fly up in the air and you land on your back, as if you'd slipped on a banana peel

blazes—2-by-6-inch paint swatches on trees that mark the trail; white blazes mark the official A.T., while blue blazes mark routes to shelters or other features

blue-blazer—hiker who shortcuts and is not committed to passing every white blaze on the A.T.

cairn—manmade pile of stones used to mark a trail in treeless areas

cathole—6- to 8-inch-deep hole for human waste a hiker digs 200 feet from any water source, camp, or trail

face plant—a face-first tumble

flip-flop—to hike a section of trail in one direction, then return to the starting point and hike in the opposite direction—*flip-flopper*

frost heave—lumps of frozen soil that jut above the surrounding ground and obstruct the trail

granny gear—a slow hiking pace

half-gallon club—membership open to any hiker who consumes an entire half-gallon of ice cream in one sitting, most often attempted at Ironmasters Mansion hostel to mark reaching the halfway point on the A.T.

hiker box—a box or bin in a shelter, hostel, or outfitter used to exchange supplies

leapfrog—a thru-hike of the A.T. in discontinuous segments

MUDs—mindless ups and downs (a short, difficult trail section)

NOBO—northbound hiker

PUDs—pointless ups and downs (an extended, difficult trail section), usually unrewarded with views

purist—a hiker committed to passing every official white blaze on the A.T.

red-blazing—hiking after a nasty, bloody tumble

register—a notebook in a shelter or other location in which hikers leave advice, quips, and other messages

ridgerunner—person paid to hike and oversee a specific section of heavily used trail during the busy season

scree—loose stones or debris on a slope or at the base of a hill or cliff

section-hike—a complete hike of the A.T. in sections over a period of years—*section-hiker*

slackpack—to hike without a pack, which is sent ahead for pick-up

SOBO—southbound hiker

stile—steps that pass over a fence or wall

switchback—a zigzag trail, built to ease passage up (and down) a steep grade

thru-hike—a more-or-less continuous hike of the entire trail—*thru-hiker*

trail angel—person who helps hikers by providing food, drinks, or rides for no fee

trail magic—serendipitous things that happen on the trail, often related to strangers sharing food and drink

trail name—a hiker's trail moniker

trudge mode—slogging pace at the end of a long day

turtle-ing—a tumble in which hiker lands on pack and struggles to regain footing

umbles—stumbles, bumbles, and mumbles that may signal a more serious malady, such as dehydration or hypothermia.

vitamin I—ibuprofen or other pain medication

web walking—to be the first hiker on the trail in the morning, thereby clearing spider webs, usually with one's face

widowmaker—dead limb that drops from a tree without warning

yellow-blazer—someone who hitchhikes around trail sections; named for highway yellow center line

Yogi-ing—begging food, as in Yogi Bear

zero day—a day off from hiking

zombie zone—a state of absent-minded hiking

ANSWERS TO QUESTIONS ON PAGE 61

1. T	2. T	3. F	4. F	5. T (and a good pair of shoes)		6. F	7. T	8. F	9. F	10. F (wintry conditions are possible)
11. b	12. d	13. d	14. d	15. d	16. d	17. d	18. c	19. b	20. a

Sunday	Monday	Tuesday	Wednesday	Thursday	Friday	Saturday

	Sunday	Monday	Tuesday	Wednesday	Thursday	Friday	Saturday

Sunday	Monday	Tuesday	Wednesday	Thursday	Friday	Saturday

Sunday	Monday	Tuesday	Wednesday	Thursday	Friday	Saturday

Sunday	Monday	Tuesday	Wednesday	Thursday	Friday	Saturday

	Sunday	Monday	Tuesday	Wednesday	Thursday	Friday	Saturday

Sunday	Monday	Tuesday	Wednesday	Thursday	Friday	Saturday

Sunday	Monday	Tuesday	Wednesday	Thursday	Friday	Saturday

Use this list as you plan your itinerary. Calculate how far you might go on a given day and where that puts you in terms of a place to sleep, then adjust, adjust, adjust. Use pencil, as you'll refer back to these pages when you plan mail drops. Shelters are listed in Roman type; locations with post offices in **boldface**; lodges, campgrounds, campsites, and other waypoints in *italics*. Listed mileages are for early 2015; if a discrepancy arises, check the current *Appalachian Trail Data Book*. A town marked with a ◆ is a designated Appalachian Trail Community™ or in a designated county. *"Miles from last shelter" includes miles on and off the A.T.; mileage to a town is to the post office.*

NORTHBOUND				SOUTHBOUND		
MILES FROM KATAHDIN	MILES FROM LAST SHELTER		MILES OFF A.T.	MILES FROM LAST SHELTER	MILES FROM SPRINGER	COMMENTS
2,189.2	1.5	*Springer Mountain Terminus*			-	
2,189.0	1.7	Springer Mountain Shelter	0.2	3.0	0.2	
2,186.4	3.0	Stover Creek Shelter	0.2	5.7	2.8	
2,181.1	5.7	Hawk Mountain Shelter	0.2	8.0	8.1	
2,173.4	8.0	Gooch Mountain Shelter	0.1	12.8	15.8	
2,168.1	7.4	**Suches, Ga.** ◆	2.0	9.4	21.1	
2,161.1	12.8	Woods Hole Shelter	0.4	1.6	28.1	
2,159.9	1.6	Blood Mountain Shelter		10.3	29.3	
2,157.5	2.4	*Neel Gap* ◆		7.9	31.7	
2,150.8	7.9	Whitley Gap Shelter	1.2	6.0	38.4	
2,146.0	6.0	Low Gap Shelter		7.3	43.2	
2,138.7	7.3	Blue Mountain Shelter		8.1	50.5	
2,136.3	11.4	**Helen, Ga.** ◆	9.0	14.7	52.9	
2,130.6	8.1	Tray Mountain Shelter	0.0	7.7	58.6	
2,123.2	7.7	Deep Gap Shelter	0.3	8.6	66.0	
2,119.6	14.9	**Hiawassee, Ga.** ◆	11.0	15.7	69.6	
2,115.1	8.6	Plumorchard Gap Shelter	0.2	7.5	74.1	
2,107.8	7.5	Muskrat Creek Shelter		4.9	81.4	
2,102.9	4.9	Standing Indian Shelter		7.6	86.3	
2,095.3	7.6	Carter Gap Shelters		8.6	93.9	
2,086.7	8.6	Long Branch Shelter		3.5	102.5	
2,083.2	3.5	Rock Gap Shelter		8.5	106.0	
2,079.4	13.8	**Franklin, N.C.** ◆	10.0	14.7	109.8	
2,075.2	8.5	Siler Bald Shelter	0.5	7.3	114.0	
2,068.4	7.3	Wayah Shelter		4.8	120.8	
2,063.6	4.8	Cold Spring Shelter		5.8	125.6	
2,057.8	5.8	Wesser Bald Shelter		4.9	131.4	
2,052.9	4.9	A. Rufus Morgan Shelter		0.8	136.3	
2,052.1	0.8	*Nantahala Outdoor Center, Wesser, N.C.*		6.9	137.1	

MILES FROM KATAHDIN	MILES FROM LAST SHELTER		MILES OFF A.T.	MILES FROM LAST SHELTER	MILES FROM SPRINGER	COMMENTS
2,045.2	6.9	Sassafras Gap Shelter		9.1	144.0	
2,036.1	9.1	Brown Fork Gap Shelter		6.1	153.1	
2,030.0	6.1	Cable Gap Shelter		6.7	159.2	
2,024.5	7.5	**Fontana Dam, N.C.**	◆ 2.0	3.2	164.7	
2,023.3	6.7	Fontana Dam Shelter		11.1	165.9	
2,012.2	11.1	Mollies Ridge Shelter		2.8	177.0	
2,009.4	2.8	Russell Field Shelter		2.9	179.8	
2,006.5	2.9	Eagle Creek Trail to				
		Spence Field Shelter	0.2	6.5	182.7	
2,000.2	6.5	Derrick Knob Shelter		5.8	189.0	
1,994.4	5.8	Silers Bald Shelter		1.7	194.8	
1,992.7	1.7	Double Spring Gap Shelter		6.8	196.5	
1,986.4	6.8	Mt. Collins Shelter	0.5	8.0	202.8	
1,981.9	20.0	**Gatlinburg, Tenn.**	15.0	18.0	207.3	
1,978.9	8.0	Icewater Spring Shelter		7.8	210.3	
1,971.5	7.8	Peck's Corner Shelter	0.4	5.6	217.7	
1,966.3	5.6	Tri-Corner Knob Shelter		7.7	222.9	
1,958.6	7.7	Cosby Knob Shelter		7.1	230.6	
1,951.5	7.1	Davenport Gap Shelter		10.7	237.7	
1,941.0	10.7	Groundhog Creek Shelter	0.2	8.4	248.2	
1,932.8	8.4	Roaring Fork Shelter		4.9	256.4	
1,927.9	4.9	Walnut Mountain Shelter		9.9	261.3	
1,918.0	9.9	Deer Park Mountain Shelter		14.2	271.2	
1,914.8	3.2	**Hot Springs, N.C.**	◆	11.0	274.4	
1,903.8	14.2	Spring Mountain Shelter		8.6	285.4	
1,895.2	8.6	Little Laurel Shelter		6.8	294.0	
1,888.4	6.8	Jerry Cabin Shelter		6.4	300.8	
1,882.0	6.4	Flint Mountain Shelter		8.9	307.2	
1,873.2	8.9	Hogback Ridge Shelter	0.1	10.2	316.0	
1,863.1	10.2	Bald Mountain Shelter		10.6	326.1	
1,852.5	10.6	No Business Knob Shelter		10.5	336.7	
1,846.2	10.1	**Erwin, Tenn.**	◆ 3.8	8.0	343.0	
1,842.0	10.5	Curley Maple Gap Shelter		12.8	347.2	
1,829.2	12.8	Cherry Gap Shelter		9.2	360.0	
1,826.1	13.4	**Unicoi, Tenn.**	10.3	16.4	363.1	
1,820.1	9.2	Clyde Smith Shelter	0.1	8.5	369.1	
1,811.7	8.5	Roan High Knob Shelter		5.2	377.5	
1,806.5	5.2	Stan Murray Shelter		2.2	382.7	
1,804.6	2.2	Overmountain Shelter	0.3	18.3	384.6	
1,795.4	12.0	**Elk Park, N.C.**	2.5	5.9	393.8	
1,795.4	5.9	**Roan Mountain, Tenn.**	3.4	12.2	393.8	
1,786.6	18.3	Mountaineer Falls Shelter		9.6	402.6	

MILES FROM KATAHDIN	MILES FROM LAST SHELTER		MILES OFF A.T.	MILES FROM LAST SHELTER	MILES FROM SPRINGER	COMMENTS
1,777.0	9.6	Moreland Gap Shelter		8.2	412.2	
1,768.8	8.2	Laurel Fork Shelter		8.6	420.4	
1,762.1	8.7	**Hampton, Tenn.**	2.0	3.9	427.1	
1,760.2	8.6	Watauga Lake Shelter		7.2	429.0	
1,753.0	7.2	Vandeventer Shelter		6.8	436.2	
1,746.2	6.8	Iron Mountain Shelter		7.6	443.0	
1,738.6	7.6	Double Springs Shelter		8.3	450.6	
1,735.1	6.2	**Shady Valley, Tenn.**	2.7	7.5	454.1	
1,730.3	8.3	Abingdon Gap Shelter		19.9	458.9	
1,720.1	10.2	**Damascus, Va.**	◆	9.7	469.1	
1,710.6	19.9	Saunders Shelter	0.2	6.5	478.6	
1,704.3	6.5	Lost Mountain Shelter		12.4	484.9	
1,691.9	12.4	Thomas Knob Shelter		5.2	497.3	
1,686.7	5.2	Wise Shelter		6.0	502.5	
1,680.7	6.0	Old Orchard Shelter		4.2	508.5	
1,676.5	4.2	Hurricane Mountain Shelter		9.0	512.7	
1,671.4	7.7	**Troutdale, Va.**	2.6	6.5	517.8	
1,667.5	9.0	Trimpi Shelter		9.8	521.7	
1,657.7	9.8	Partnership Shelter		6.7	531.5	
1,657.6	3.3	**Sugar Grove, Va.**	3.2	9.8	531.6	
1,651.0	6.7	Chatfield Shelter		18.9	538.2	
1,646.5	7.7	**Atkins, Va.**	3.2	17.6	542.7	
1,632.1	18.9	Knot Maul Branch Shelter		9.4	557.1	
1,622.7	9.4	Chestnut Knob Shelter		10.6	566.5	
1,612.1	10.6	Jenkins Shelter		15.6	577.1	
1,600.0	14.8	**Bland, Va.**	◆ 2.7	5.2	589.2	
1,600.0	5.2	**Bastian, Va.**	2.5	6.0	589.2	
1,596.8	15.6	Helveys Mill Shelter	0.3	10.0	592.4	
1,587.1	10.0	Jenny Knob Shelter		14.5	602.1	
1,572.6	14.5	Wapiti Shelter		9.5	616.6	
1,563.1	9.5	Doc's Knob Shelter		15.7	626.1	
1,554.3	9.8	**Pearisburg, Va.**	◆ 1.0	7.9	634.9	
1,547.4	15.7	Rice Field Shelter		12.6	641.8	
1,534.8	12.6	Pine Swamp Branch Shelter		3.9	654.4	
1,530.9	3.9	Bailey Gap Shelter		8.8	658.3	
1,522.1	8.8	War Spur Shelter		5.8	667.1	
1,516.3	5.8	Laurel Creek Shelter		6.7	672.9	
1,509.9	6.7	Sarver Hollow Shelter	0.3	6.3	679.3	
1,503.9	6.3	Niday Shelter		10.4	685.3	
1,493.8	10.4	Pickle Branch Shelter	0.3	13.9	695.4	
1,481.2	13.9	**Catawba, Va.**	1.0	2.0	708.0	
1,480.2	13.9	Johns Spring Shelter		1.0	709.0	

MILES FROM KATAHDIN	MILES FROM LAST SHELTER		MILES OFF A.T.	MILES FROM LAST SHELTER	MILES FROM SPRINGER	COMMENTS
1,479.2	1.0	Catawba Mountain Shelter		2.4	710.0	
1,476.8	2.4	Campbell Shelter		6.0	712.4	
1,470.8	6.0	Lamberts Meadow Shelter		14.4	718.4	
1,461.4	11.7	**Cloverdale, Va.**	2.3	3.3	727.8	
1,461.4	3.3	**Daleville, Va.**	1.0	3.3	727.8	
1,459.9	3.3	**Troutville, Va.** ◆	0.8	4.3	729.3	
1,456.4	14.4	Fullhardt Knob Shelter		6.2	732.8	
1,450.2	6.2	Wilson Creek Shelter		7.5	739.0	
1,442.9	7.5	Bobblets Gap Shelter	0.2	6.7	746.3	
1,439.8	8.3	**Buchanan, Va.**	5.0	8.4	749.4	
1,436.4	6.7	Cove Mountain Shelter		7.0	752.8	
1,429.4	7.0	Bryant Ridge Shelter		4.9	759.8	
1,424.5	4.9	Cornelius Creek Shelter		5.3	764.7	
1,419.2	5.3	Thunder Hill Shelter		12.4	770.0	
1,406.8	12.4	Matts Creek Shelter		3.9	782.4	
1,404.6	8.3	**Glasgow, Va.** ◆	6.1	7.8	784.6	
1,402.9	3.9	Johns Hollow Shelter		9.0	786.3	
1,394.1	9.0	Punchbowl Shelter	0.2	9.7	795.1	
1,384.6	9.7	Brown Mountain Creek Shelter		6.2	804.6	
1,382.8	11.5	**Buena Vista, Va.** ◆	9.7	14.1	806.4	
1,379.0	6.2	Cow Camp Gap Shelter	0.6	10.8	810.2	
1,368.8	10.8	Seeley-Woodworth Shelter		6.6	820.4	
1,366.5	4.8	**Montebello, Va.**	2.5	6.8	822.7	
1,362.2	6.6	The Priest Shelter		7.6	827.0	
1,354.6	7.6	Harpers Creek Shelter		6.2	834.6	
1,348.4	6.2	Maupin Field Shelter		15.8	840.8	
1,332.6	15.8	Paul C. Wolfe Shelter		13.0	856.6	
1,327.6	9.5	**Waynesboro, Va.** ◆	4.5	12.5	861.6	
1,319.9	13.0	Calf Mountain Shelter	0.3	13.5	869.3	
1,306.9	13.5	Blackrock Hut	0.2	13.5	882.3	
1,293.7	13.5	Pinefield Hut	0.1	8.4	895.5	
1,285.5	8.4	Hightop Hut	0.1	12.6	903.7	
1,282.1	11.0	**Elkton, Va.**	7.5	16.6	907.1	
1,273.1	12.6	Bearfence Mountain Hut	0.1	11.8	916.1	
1,261.6	11.8	Rock Spring Hut	0.2	11.1	927.6	
1,250.7	11.1	Byrds Nest #3 Shelter		4.6	938.5	
1,247.5	8.8	**Luray, Va.** ◆	5.6	7.0	941.7	
1,246.3	4.6	Pass Mountain Hut	0.2	13.5	942.9	
1,233.2	13.5	Gravel Springs Hut	0.2	10.7	956.0	
1,222.7	10.7	Tom Floyd Wayside		8.1	966.5	
1,219.8	6.1	**Front Royal, Va.** ◆	3.2	8.4	969.4	
1,214.6	8.1	Jim and Molly Denton Shelter		5.5	974.6	

MILES FROM KATAHDIN	MILES FROM LAST SHELTER		MILES OFF A.T.	MILES FROM LAST SHELTER	MILES FROM SPRINGER	COMMENTS
1,213.5	2.2	**Linden, Va.**	1.1	5.5	975.7	
1,209.1	5.5	Manassas Gap Shelter		4.7	980.1	
1,204.6	4.7	Dick's Dome Shelter	0.2	8.8	984.6	
1,196.2	8.8	Rod Hollow Shelter	0.2	7.1	993.0	
1,189.3	7.1	Sam Moore Shelter		11.2	999.9	
1,185.7	5.3	**Bluemont, Va.**	1.7	9.3	1,003.5	
1,178.3	11.2	*Blackburn Trail Center*	0.2	3.5	1,010.9	
1,175.1	3.5	David Lesser Memorial Shelter	0.1	15.8	1,014.1	
1,166.5	9.2	**Harpers Ferry, W.Va.** ◆	0.5	7.6	1,022.7	
1,159.5	15.8	Ed Garvey Shelter	0.1	4.5	1,029.7	
1,155.4	4.5	Crampton Gap Shelter	0.3	5.5	1,033.8	
1,150.4	5.5	Rocky Run Shelter	0.2	7.8	1,038.8	
1,148.4	4.6	**Boonsboro, Md.**	2.4	8.0	1,040.8	
1,142.9	7.8	Pine Knob Shelter	0.1	8.3	1,046.3	
1,134.9	10.5	**Smithsburg, Md.**	2.4	2.6	1,054.3	
1,134.7	8.3	Ensign Cowall Shelter		5.1	1,054.5	
1,129.8	5.1	Raven Rock Shelter	0.2	9.8	1,059.4	
1,125.1	6.5	**Cascade, Md.**	1.6	5.6	1,064.1	
1,122.3	5.6	**Blue Ridge Summit, Pa.** ◆	1.2	3.3	1,066.9	
1,120.2	9.8	Deer Lick Shelters		2.4	1,069.0	
1,117.8	2.4	Antietam Shelter		1.2	1,071.4	
1,116.6	1.2	Tumbling Run Shelters		6.8	1,072.6	
1,111.7	6.1	**South Mountain, Pa.**	1.2	3.1	1,077.5	
1,110.0	6.8	Rocky Mountain Shelters	0.2	5.8	1,079.2	
1,107.0	6.7	**Fayetteville, Pa.**	3.5	6.1	1,082.2	
1,104.4	5.8	Quarry Gap Shelters		7.4	1,084.8	
1,097.0	7.4	Birch Run Shelter		2.4	1,092.2	
1,094.6	2.4	HALFWAY		3.8	1,094.6	
1,090.8	3.8	Toms Run Shelter		11.1	1,098.4	
1,079.9	11.1	James Fry (Tagg Run) Shelter	0.2	8.5	1,109.3	
1,076.7	5.9	**Mt. Holly Springs, Pa.**	2.5	7.6	1,112.5	
1,071.8	8.5	Alec Kennedy Shelter	0.2	18.4	1,117.4	
1,067.9	4.1	**Boiling Springs, Pa.** ◆		14.3	1,121.3	
1,053.6	18.4	Darlington Shelter		7.3	1,135.6	
1,046.3	7.3	Cove Mountain Shelter		8.3	1,142.9	
1,042.2	4.1	**Duncannon, Pa.** ◆		4.2	1,147.0	
1,038.0	8.3	Clarks Ferry Shelter		6.7	1,151.2	
1,031.3	6.7	Peters Mountain Shelter		18.3	1,157.9	
1,013.3	18.3	Rausch Gap Shelter	0.3	13.7	1,175.9	
999.9	13.7	William Penn Shelter		4.2	1,189.3	
995.8	4.2	501 Shelter	0.1	15.5	1,193.4	
995.8	3.8	**Pine Grove, Pa.**	3.7	19.1	1,193.4	

MILES FROM KATAHDIN	MILES FROM LAST SHELTER		MILES OFF A.T.	MILES FROM LAST SHELTER	MILES FROM SPRINGER	COMMENTS
980.7	15.5	Eagle's Nest Shelter	0.3	15.0	1,208.5	
972.1	8.9	**Port Clinton, Pa.**		4.2	1,217.1	
971.4	4.2	**Hamburg, Pa.**	3.5	8.9	1,217.8	
966.0	15.0	Windsor Furnace Shelter		9.3	1,223.2	
956.9	9.3	Eckville Shelter	0.2	7.6	1,232.3	
949.5	7.6	Allentown Hiking Club Shelter		10.0	1,239.7	
939.5	10.0	Bake Oven Knob Shelter		6.8	1,249.7	
932.7	6.8	George W. Outerbridge Shelter		16.8	1,256.5	
932.1	2.6	**Slatington, Pa.**	2.0	4.3	1,257.1	
931.8	4.3	**Walnutport, Pa.**	2.0	4.0	1,257.4	
931.8	4.0	**Palmerton, Pa.**	2.0	8.5	1,257.4	
926.8	8.5	**Danielsville, Pa.**	1.5	12.4	1,262.4	
916.0	16.8	Leroy A. Smith Shelter	0.1	13.9	1,273.2	
911.4	5.7	**Wind Gap, Pa.** ◆	1.0	10.2	1,277.8	
902.2	13.9	Kirkridge Shelter		31.4	1,287.0	
895.8	6.5	**Delaware Water Gap, Pa.** ◆	0.1	25.1	1,293.4	
871.0	31.4	Brink Road Shelter	0.2	6.9	1,318.2	
867.4	7.2	**Branchville, N.J.**	3.4	6.5	1,321.8	
864.4	6.9	Gren Anderson Shelter	0.1	5.9	1,324.8	
858.6	5.9	Mashipacong Shelter		3.0	1,330.6	
856.0	3.0	Rutherford Shelter	0.4	5.1	1,333.2	
851.4	5.1	High Point Shelter	0.1	12.5	1,337.8	
844.3	7.6	**Unionville, N.Y.**	0.4	5.7	1,344.9	
839.0	12.5	Pochuck Mountain Shelter		11.6	1,350.2	
836.3	3.8	**Glenwood, N.J.**	1.1	7.3	1,352.9	
832.5	7.3	**Vernon, N.J.**	2.4	7.5	1,356.7	
827.5	11.6	Wawayanda Shelter	0.1	12.2	1,361.7	
817.5	12.1	**Greenwood Lake, N.Y.**	2.0	4.1	1,371.7	
815.4	12.2	Wildcat Shelter		14.3	1,373.8	
801.1	14.3	Fingerboard Shelter		5.3	1,388.1	
795.8	5.3	William Brien Memorial Shelter		3.6	1,393.4	
792.6	3.6	West Mountain Shelter	0.4	32.6	1,396.6	
786.4	6.6	**Bear Mountain, N.Y.**		1.7	1,402.8	
785.6	1.7	**Ft. Montgomery, N.Y.**	0.9	11.2	1,403.6	
779.8	11.2	**Peekskill, N.Y.**	4.5	23.9	1,409.4	
760.4	32.6	RPH Shelter		9.0	1,428.8	
755.3	6.9	**Stormville, N.Y.**	1.8	5.7	1,433.9	
751.4	9.0	Morgan Stewart Shelter		7.8	1,437.8	
748.1	5.4	**Poughquag, N.Y.**	2.1	6.6	1,441.1	
743.6	7.8	Telephone Pioneers Shelter		8.8	1,445.6	
742.9	3.8	**Pawling, N.Y.** ◆	3.1	11.2	1,446.3	
734.8	8.8	Wiley Shelter		4.0	1,454.4	

MILES FROM KATAHDIN	MILES FROM LAST SHELTER		MILES OFF A.T.	MILES FROM LAST SHELTER	MILES FROM SPRINGER	COMMENTS
733.6	4.5	**Wingdale, N.Y.**	3.3	6.5	1,455.6	
732.9	6.5	**Gaylordsville, Conn.**	2.5	4.6	1,456.3	
730.8	4.0	Ten Mile River Shelter		8.4	1,458.4	
722.4	8.4	Mt. Algo Shelter		7.3	1,466.8	
722.1	1.1	**Kent, Conn.**	0.8	7.8	1,467.1	
715.1	7.3	Stewart Hollow Brook Shelter		10.0	1,474.1	
711.0	5.0	**Cornwall Bridge, Conn.**	0.9	7.9	1,478.2	
706.2	7.9	**West Cornwall, Conn.**	2.2	3.3	1,483.0	
705.1	10.0	Pine Swamp Brook Shelter		11.9	1,484.1	
697.0	8.6	**Falls Village, Conn.**	0.5	4.3	1,492.2	
693.7	11.9	Limestone Spring Shelter	0.5	8.0	1,495.5	
690.3	4.3	**Salisbury, Conn.**	0.4	4.5	1,498.9	
686.2	8.0	Riga Shelter		1.2	1,503.0	
685.0	1.2	Brassie Brook Shelter		8.8	1,504.2	
676.2	8.8	The Hemlocks Shelter		0.1	1,513.0	
676.1	0.1	Glen Brook Shelter		14.3	1,513.1	
671.8	5.5	**South Egremont, Mass.**	1.2	8.0	1,517.4	
668.2	8.0	**Sheffield, Mass.**	3.2	5.0	1,521.0	
668.2	5.0	**Great Barrington, Mass.** ◆	1.8	8.2	1,521.0	
661.8	14.3	Tom Leonard Shelter		5.3	1,527.4	
659.8	6.3	**Monterey, Mass.**	4.3	7.6	1,529.4	
656.5	5.3	Mt. Wilcox South Shelter		2.1	1,532.7	
654.7	2.1	Mt. Wilcox North Shelter	0.3	14.8	1,534.5	
648.8	6.8	**Tyringham, Mass.**	0.6	9.2	1,540.4	
640.7	14.8	*Upper Goose Pond Cabin*	0.5	9.3	1,548.5	
639.1	7.1	**Lee, Mass.**	5.0	12.2	1,550.1	
631.9	12.2	October Mountain Shelter		9.0	1,557.3	
629.7	7.2	**Becket, Mass.**	5.0	11.8	1,559.5	
623.1	9.0	Kay Wood Shelter	0.2	17.3	1,566.1	
620.1	3.2	**Dalton, Mass.**		9.0	1,569.1	
611.1	9.0	**Cheshire, Mass.**		4.5	1,578.1	
610.6	4.5	**Adams, Mass.**	4.0	8.6	1,578.6	
606.2	17.3	Mark Noepel Shelter	0.2	7.1	1,583.0	
599.6	7.1	Wilbur Clearing Shelter	0.3	10.4	1,589.6	
596.6	5.8	**North Adams, Mass.**	2.5	5.1	1,592.6	
596.6	5.1	**Williamstown, Mass.**	2.6	9.7	1,592.6	
589.7	10.4	Seth Warner Shelter	0.2	7.4	1,599.5	
582.5	7.4	Congdon Shelter		5.9	1,606.7	
578.2	9.4	**Bennington, Vt.**	5.1	6.7	1,611.0	
576.6	5.9	Melville Nauheim Shelter		8.5	1,612.6	
568.1	8.5	Goddard Shelter		4.3	1,621.1	
563.8	4.3	Kid Gore Shelter		4.6	1,625.4	

MILES FROM KATAHDIN	MILES FROM LAST SHELTER		MILES OFF A.T.	MILES FROM LAST SHELTER	MILES FROM SPRINGER	COMMENTS
559.2	4.6	Story Spring Shelter		10.5	1,630.0	
548.8	10.5	Stratton Pond Shelter	0.1	5.5	1,640.4	
543.9	5.5	William B. Douglas Shelter	0.5	3.6	1,645.3	
540.9	3.6	Spruce Peak Shelter	0.1	5.0	1,648.3	
538.1	8.4	**Manchester Center, Vt.**	5.5	7.6	1,651.1	
536.1	5.0	Bromley Shelter	0.1	8.2	1,653.1	
528.0	8.2	Peru Peak Shelter		4.7	1,661.2	
523.3	4.7	Lost Pond Shelter		2.5	1,665.9	
521.8	2.5	Old Job Shelter	1.0	1.2	1,667.4	
521.6	1.2	Big Branch Shelter		3.3	1,667.6	
520.3	4.8	**Danby, Vt.**	3.5	5.5	1,668.9	
518.3	3.3	Little Rock Pond Shelter		5.0	1,670.9	
513.5	5.0	Greenwall Shelter	0.2	5.3	1,675.7	
512.0	4.5	**Wallingford, Vt.**	2.8	6.4	1,677.2	
508.4	5.3	Minerva Hinchey Shelter		3.8	1,680.8	
504.7	3.8	Clarendon Shelter	0.1	5.9	1,684.5	
498.9	5.9	Governor Clement Shelter		4.3	1,690.3	
494.6	4.3	Cooper Lodge		3.0	1,694.6	
492.1	3.0	Sherburne Pass Trail to Pico Camp	0.5	2.5	1,697.1	
490.2	2.5	Churchill Scott Shelter	0.1	12.1	1,699.0	
488.3	10.6	**Rutland, Vt.**	8.6	12.5	1,700.9	
485.0	12.5	**Killington, Vt.**	0.6	7.4	1,704.2	
478.3	12.1	Stony Brook Shelter	0.1	10.2	1,710.9	
468.4	10.2	Wintturi Shelter	0.2	11.9	1,720.8	
464.6	8.4	**Woodstock, Vt.**	4.4	6.8	1,724.6	
463.1	6.8	**South Pomfret, Vt.**	0.9	7.3	1,726.1	
456.8	11.9	Thistle Hill Shelter	0.1	9.0	1,732.4	
452.0	11.9	**Hartford, Vt.**	7.0	11.1	1,737.2	
448.0	9.0	Happy Hill Shelter	0.1	7.6	1,741.2	
443.7	4.7	**Norwich, Vt.** ◆	0.3	1.8	1,745.5	
442.2	1.8	**Hanover, N.H.** ◆		1.7	1,747.0	
440.7	7.6	Velvet Rocks Shelter	0.2	9.7	1,748.5	
431.2	9.7	Moose Mountain Shelter		5.9	1,758.0	
425.5	5.9	Trapper John Shelter	0.2	6.9	1,763.7	
424.6	4.3	**Lyme, N.H.**	3.2	9.0	1,764.6	
418.8	6.9	*Firewarden's Cabin and Fire Tower*		5.6	1,770.4	
413.5	5.6	Hexacuba Shelter	0.3	16.0	1,775.7	
408.6	10.0	**Wentworth, N.H.**	4.8	13.6	1,780.6	
403.8	13.6	**Warren, N.H.**	4.0	9.3	1,785.4	
398.9	9.3	**Glencliff, N.H.**	0.4	1.5	1,790.3	
397.8	16.0	Jeffers Brook Shelter		6.9	1,791.4	
390.9	6.9	Beaver Brook Shelter/Campsite		9.0	1,798.3	

MILES FROM KATAHDIN	MILES FROM LAST SHELTER		MILES OFF A.T.	MILES FROM LAST SHELTER	MILES FROM SPRINGER	COMMENTS
389.4	6.5	**North Woodstock, N.H.**	5.0	12.5	1,799.8	
381.9	9.0	Eliza Brook Shelter/Campsite		4.1	1,807.3	
377.9	4.1	Kinsman Pond Shelter/Campsite	0.1	2.0	1,811.3	
376.0	2.0	*Lonesome Lake Hut*		5.5	1,813.2	
373.1	10.2	**Lincoln, N.H.**	7.3	9.9	1,816.1	
370.5	5.5	*Liberty Spring Tentsite*		4.9	1,818.7	
366.7	4.9	*Greenleaf Hut*	1.1	5.1	1,822.5	
362.8	5.1	Garfield Ridge Shelter/Campsite	0.1	2.8	1,826.4	
360.1	2.8	*Galehead Hut*		3.6	1,829.1	
357.3	3.6	Guyot Shelter/Campsite	0.8	5.0	1,831.9	
353.1	5.0	*Zealand Falls Hut*		4.8	1,836.1	
348.3	4.8	Ethan Pond Shelter/Campsite		9.3	1,840.9	
345.4	12.9	**Bartlett, N.H.**	10.0	16.4	1,843.8	
339.0	9.3	*Mizpah Spring Hut,* Nauman Tentsite		4.7	1,850.2	
334.3	4.7	*Lakes of the Clouds Hut*		3.4	1,854.9	
332.9	3.4	Hermit Lake Shelter/Campsite	2.0	7.1	1,856.3	
328.7	7.1	The Perch Shelter/Campsite	0.9	2.7	1,860.5	
328.1	2.7	Gray Knob Cabin	1.2	2.1	1,861.1	
327.2	2.1	*Madison Spring Hut*		7.8	1,862.0	
319.4	7.8	*Pinkham Notch*		6.1	1,869.8	
313.5	6.1	*Carter Notch Hut*	0.2	7.6	1,875.7	
306.3	7.6	Imp Shelter/Campsite	0.2	6.3	1,882.9	
300.2	6.3	Rattle River Shelter/Campsite		13.9	1,889.0	
298.3	5.5	**Gorham, N.H.**	3.6	15.6	1,890.9	
286.5	13.9	Gentian PondShelter/Campsite	0.2	5.7	1,902.7	
281.3	5.7	Carlo Col Shelter/Campsite	0.3	4.7	1,907.9	
276.9	4.7	Full Goose Shelter/Campsite		5.1	1,912.3	
271.8	5.1	Speck Pond Shelter/Campsite		6.9	1,917.4	
264.9	6.9	Baldpate Lean-to		3.5	1,924.3	
261.4	3.5	Frye Notch Lean-to		10.5	1,927.8	
256.9	12.5	**Andover, Maine**	8.0	14.0	1,932.3	
250.9	10.5	Hall Mountain Lean-to		12.8	1,938.3	
246.8	13.1	**Andover, Maine**	9.0	17.7	1,942.4	
238.1	12.8	Bemis Mountain Lean-to		8.3	1,951.1	
233.5	15.6	**Oquossoc, Maine**	11.0	14.7	1,955.7	
229.8	8.3	Sabbath Day Pond Lean-to		11.2	1,959.4	
220.4	18.4	**Rangeley, Maine** ◆	9.0	10.8	1,968.8	
218.6	11.2	Piazza Rock Lean-to		8.9	1,970.6	
209.7	8.9	Poplar Ridge Lean-to		8.0	1,979.5	
201.7	8.0	Spaulding Mountain Lean-to		18.6	1,987.5	
188.2	18.5	**Stratton, Maine**	5.0	10.1	2,001.0	
183.1	18.6	Horns Pond Lean-tos		10.2	2,006.1	

	NORTHBOUND				SOUTHBOUND		
MILES FROM KATAHDIN	MILES FROM LAST SHELTER		MILES OFF A.T.	MILES FROM LAST SHELTER	MILES FROM SPRINGER	COMMENTS
172.9	10.2	Little Bigelow Lean-to		7.7	2,016.3	
165.2	7.7	West Carry Pond Lean-to		10.0	2,024.0	
155.2	10.0	Pierce Pond Lean-to		9.7	2,034.0	
151.2	4.3	**Caratunk, Maine**	0.3	6.0	2,038.0	
145.5	9.7	Pleasant Pond Lean-to		9.0	2,043.7	
136.5	9.0	Bald Mountain Brook Lean-to		4.1	2,052.7	
132.4	4.1	Moxie Bald Lean-to		8.9	2,056.8	
123.5	8.9	Horseshoe Canyon Lean-to		12.0	2,065.7	
114.5	13.0	**Monson, Maine** ◆	4.0	7.0	2,074.7	
111.5	12.0	Leeman Brook Lean-to		7.4	2,077.7	
104.1	7.4	Wilson Valley Lean-to		4.7	2,085.1	
99.4	4.7	Long Pond Stream Lean-to		4.4	2,089.8	
95.4	4.4	Cloud Pond Lean-to	0.4	7.3	2,093.8	
88.5	7.3	Chairback Gap Lean-to		9.9	2,100.7	
78.6	9.9	Carl A. Newhall Lean-to		7.2	2,110.6	
71.4	7.2	Logan Brook Lean-to		3.6	2,117.8	
67.8	3.6	East Branch Lean-to		8.1	2,121.4	
59.7	8.1	Cooper Brook Falls Lean-to		11.4	2,129.5	
48.3	11.4	Potaywadjo Spring Lean-to		10.1	2,140.9	
38.2	10.1	Wadleigh Stream Lean-to		8.1	2,151.0	
30.1	8.1	Rainbow Stream Lean-to		11.5	2,159.1	
18.6	11.5	Hurd Brook Lean-to		11.2	2,170.6	
7.5	11.2	*Daicey Pond Campground*	0.1	2.3	2,181.7	
5.2	2.3	Katahdin Stream Cmpgrnd, The Birches	0.3	-	2,184.0	
-	-	***Katahdin (Baxter Peak terminus)***			2,189.2	

Thru-Hike Budget

Use this worksheet to rough out the most basic of thru-hike budgets. There are many variables, and you'll go through several iterations of this budget before you have a true sense of how much you'll spend. Use the space at the bottom of the page for calculations.

Transportation (to trailheads; shuttles)   _____

Food   _____

Gear

      Shoes/Boots   _____

      Backpack   _____

      Tent   _____

      Sleeping Bag   _____

      Clothing   _____

      Stove   _____

      Miscellany   _____

      Replacement Gear   _____

Lodging/Restaurants   _____

Laundry   _____

Entertainment   _____

Mail Drops   _____

TOTAL   _____

Gear Checklist

◗ ESSENTIAL

_____ shoes/boots
_____ socks
_____ backpack
_____ hydration system
_____ pack cover
_____ tent/tarp
_____ sleeping bag
_____ stuff sack
_____ nylon cord
_____ underwear/sports bra
_____ shirts, shorts, pants
_____ sweater/pullover
_____ raingear
_____ hat/gloves
_____ bandanna
_____ sunglasses & eyeglasses
_____ knife/multitool
_____ stove
_____ matches/lighter
_____ cookware
_____ water bag
_____ water filter/purifier
_____ flashlight/headlamp
_____ maps
_____ batteries
_____ whistle
_____ toilet paper
_____ trowel (for digging catholes)
_____ resealable plastic bags
_____ soap & travel towel
_____ toothbrush, paste & floss
_____ comb
_____ sunscreen
_____ lip balm
_____ first-aid kit
_____ tweezers (to remove ticks)
_____ ID (driver's license)
_____ money
_____ credit/debit card
_____ pen/pencil

_____ vitamins
_____ insect repellent

◗ USEFUL

_____ gaiters
_____ tent-repair kit
_____ sleeping pad
_____ hiking stick/trekking poles
_____ stove-repair kit
_____ candle
_____ plastic garbage bags
_____ telephone card
_____ digital camera
_____ solar battery charger
_____ journal
_____ postcards
_____ guidebooks
_____ compass/GPS
_____ rubbing alcohol/foot powder
_____ nail clippers

◗ OPTIONAL

_____ town clothes
_____ camp shoes
_____ coffee supplies
_____ BakePacker
_____ hammock
_____ travel chess set
_____ playing cards
_____ monocular/binoculars
_____ trail mascot

Food Checklist

Following are lists of suggested food items by meal, including lists of popular snacks, spices, condiments, and drinks. While amounts are largely determined by one's size and appetite, you'll need to consume a minimum of 2 pounds of food per day to replace the estimated 4,000 calories a day you'll burn while thru-hiking.

For more information and advice, pick up a copy of Lou Adsmond's *The Appalachian Trail Food Planner* (see page 56).

◗ BREAKFAST
_____ multivitamin
_____ bagel & cream cheese
_____ Carnation instant breakfast
_____ Cream of Wheat
_____ granola/breakfast bar
_____ instant oatmeal
_____ Pop-Tarts

◗ LUNCH
_____ bread
_____ cheese
_____ honey
_____ peanut butter
_____ sardines
_____ tuna

◗ DINNER
_____ dehydrated/fresh vegetables
_____ dried soup mix
_____ dried/packaged meats
_____ macaroni & cheese
_____ mashed potatoes
_____ pasta/noodles
_____ pepperoni
_____ rice
_____ sausages

◗ SPICES & CONDIMENTS
_____ salt
_____ pepper
_____ curry
_____ garlic powder
_____ Italian seasoning
_____ ketchup/mustard packets
_____ parsley
_____ squeeze margarine

◗ SNACKS
_____ candy bar
_____ cookies
_____ crackers
_____ dried/fresh fruit
_____ jerky
_____ trail mix

◗ DRINKS
_____ water (thru-hikers should drink a minimum of 1 gallon of water per day)
_____ coffee/tea
_____ powdered cocoa/hot chocolate
_____ powdered milk
_____ sports drink

Use this guide/worksheet (based on 2015 mileages) in conjunction with the rough schedule you started in the Itinerary chapter to coordinate your sleeping and resupply plans. Three hiking speeds are listed below for variations among hikers and regions; it's best to both underestimate your pace and allow time for getting into town; *miles to/from town are included in the estimates.* Check

Northbound							Southbound			
DAYS FROM LAST DROP AT...			TRAIL MILES FROM				TRAIL MILES FROM	DAYS FROM LAST DROP AT...		
8	12	15				OFF		8	12	15
MILES PER DAY			KATAHDIN	DROP POINT	ZIP CODE	A.T.	SPRINGER	MILES PER DAY		
			2,198.0	Amicalola Falls State Park	30534		8.8	I	I	I
I	I	I	2,189.2	Springer Mountain Terminus			-	3	2	2
3	2	2	2,168.1	Suches, Ga.	30572	2.0	21.1	I	I	I
I	I	I	2,157.2	**Neel Gap, Walasi-Yi Center**	30562		32.0	4	2	2
4	2	2	2,136.3	Helen, Ga.	30545	9.0	52.9	3	2	2
3	2	2	2,119.6	Hiawassee, Ga.	30546	11.0	69.6	6	4	3
6	4	3	2,079.4	Franklin, N.C.	28734	10.0	109.8	3	2	2
3	2	2	2,052.1	Nantahala Outdoor Center	28713		137.1	4	2	2
4	2	2	2,024.5	**Fontana Dam, N.C.**	28733	1.8	164.7	7	5	4
7	5	4	1,981.9	Gatlinburg, Tenn.	37738	15.0	207.3	4	3	2
4	3	2	1,914.8	**Hot Springs, N.C.**	28743		274.4	9	6	5
9	6	5	1,846.2	**Erwin, Tenn.**	37650	3.8	343.0	3	2	2
3	2	2	1,822.0	Greasy Creek Gap, Greasy Creek Friendly	28705	0.6	367.2	4	2	2
4	2	2	1,795.4	Roan Mountain, Tenn.	37687	3.4	393.8	0	0	0
0	0	0	1,795.4	Elk Park, N.C.	28622	2.5	393.8	3	2	2
3	2	2	1,770.7	Dennis Cove Road, Kincora Hostel,	37658	0.2	418.5	0	0	0
0	0	0	1,770.7	Black Bear Resort	37658	0.4	418.5	I	I	I
I	I	I	1,762.1	Hampton, Tenn.	37658	2.0	427.1	5	4	3
5	4	3	1,720.1	**Damascus, Va.**	24236		469.1	6	4	3
6	4	3	1,671.4	Troutdale, Va.	24378	2.6	517.8	2	I	I
2	I	I	1,657.6	Sugar Grove, Va.	24375	3.2	531.6	2	I	I
2	I	I	1,646.5	Va. 683, U.S. 11, I-81; Atkins, Va.	24368	3.2	542.7	6	4	3
6	4	3	1,600.0	Bastian, Va.	24314	2.7	589.2	0	0	0
0	0	0	1,600.0	Bland, Va.	24315	2.5	589.2	6	4	3
6	4	3	1,554.3	**Pearisburg, Va.**	24134	1.0	634.9	9	6	5
9	6	5	1,481.2	Catawba, Va.	24070	1.0	708.0	2	2	I
2	2	I	1,461.4	U.S. 220, I-81, Interchange Area	24083		727.8	0	0	0
0	0	0	1,459.9	**Troutville, Va.**	24175	1.3	729.3	3	2	2
3	2	2	1,439.8	Buchanan, Va.	24066	4.4	749.4	5	3	3
5	3	3	1,404.6	Glasgow, Va.	24555	5.9	784.6	I	0	0
I	0	0	1,404.6	Big Island, Va.	24526	5.1	784.6	4	3	2
4	3	2	1,382.8	Buena Vista, Va.	24416	9.3	806.4	2	2	I

your estimated pace based on elevation profiles, fitness, and goals. Distances and services are based on the 2015 *Appalachian Trail Data Book*—please check the current edition and a guidebook before using this list for planning purposes (a "restaurant" could be a diner, for example). The "accepts packages" column refers to hiker-friendly businesses in places that may or may not have post offices—refer to the current *Appalachian Trail Thru-Hikers' Companion*. "Deluxe" lodging means rooms for more than $100.

POST OFFICE	ACCEPTS PACKAGES	CONVENIENCE STORE	GROCERY/ SUPERMARKET	PLACE(S) TO EAT	HOSTEL	INEXPENSIVE LODGING	DELUXE LODGING	COMMENTS
	•			🍴			🏨 $	
⊏	•	•	🛒		🛏			
	•	•	🛒		🛏	🛏		
⊏	•	•	🛒	🍴		🏨	🏨 $	
⊏	•	•	🛒	🍴	🛏	🏨		
⊏	•	•	🛒	🍴	🛏	🏨		
	•		🛒	🍴	🛏	🏨		
⊏	•	•	🛒	🍴		🏨	🏨 $	
⊏	•	•	🛒	🍴		🏨	🏨 $	
⊏	•	•	🛒	🍴	🛏	🏨	🏨 $	
⊏	•	•	🛒	🍴	🛏	🏨	🏨 $	
	•			🍴	🛏			
⊏	•	•	🛒	🍴	🛏		🏨 $	
⊏	•			🍴				
	•		🛒		🛏			
	•		🛒			🏨		
⊏	•	•	🛒	🍴	🛏	🏨	🏨 $	
⊏	•	•	🛒	🍴	🛏	🏨	🏨 $	
⊏	•	•		🍴	🛏	🏨		
⊏			🛒					
⊏	•	•	🛒	🍴		🏨		
⊏								
⊏	•	•	🛒	🍴				
⊏	•	•	🛒	🍴	🛏	🏨		
⊏	•		🛒	🍴	🛏			
⊏	•	•	🛒	🍴		🏨		
⊏			🛒	🍴				
⊏				🍴		🏨		
⊏	•		🛒	🍴	🛏			
⊏			🛒	🍴				
✉	•	•	🛒		🛏	🏨		

8	12	15	TRAIL MILES FROM	DROP POINT	ZIP CODE	OFF A.T.	TRAIL MILES FROM	8	12	15
MILES PER DAY		KATAHDIN				SPRINGER		MILES PER DAY		
2	2	1	1,366.5	Montebello, Va.	24564	2.5	822.7	5	4	3
5	4	3	1,327.6	**Waynesboro, Va.**	22980	4.5	861.6	14	9	7
14	9	7	1,219.8	Front Royal, Va.	22630	4.2	969.4	1	1	0
1	1	0	1,213.5	Linden, Va.	22642	1.0	975.7	4	2	2
4	2	2	1,186.3	Bears Den Hostel/Bluemont, Va.	20135	1.6	1,002.9	3	2	1
3	2	1	1,166.5	**Harpers Ferry, W.Va.**	25425	0.5	1,022.7	0	0	0
0	0	0	1,166.5	**ATC Visitors Center**		0.2	1,022.7	3	2	1
3	2	1	1,148.4	Boonsboro, Md.	21713	2.4	1,040.8	2	1	1
2	1	1	1,134.9	Smithsburg, Md.	21783	2.4	1,054.3	2	1	1
2	1	1	1,122.3	Blue Ridge Summit, Pa.	17214	1.2	1,066.9	1	1	1
1	1	1	1,111.7	South Mountain, Pa.	17261	1.2	1,077.5	1	1	1
1	1	1	1,107.0	Fayetteville, Pa.	17222	3.5	1,082.2	4	3	2
4	3	2	1,076.7	Mt. Holly Springs, Pa.	17065	2.5	1,112.5	1	1	1
1	1	1	1,067.9	Boiling Springs, Pa. (ATC Regional Office)	17007		1,121.3	3	2	1
3	2	2	1,042.2	**Duncannon, Pa.**	17020		1,147.0	6	4	3
6	4	3	995.8	**Pine Grove, Pa.**	17963	3.7	1,193.4	3	2	2
3	2	2	972.1	**Port Clinton, Pa.**	19549		1,217.1	5	4	3
5	4	3	932.1	Slatington, Pa.	18080	2.0	1,257.1	0	0	0
0	0	0	931.8	Palmerton, Pa.	18071	2.0	1,257.4	3	2	1
3	2	1	911.4	Wind Gap, Pa.	18091	1.0	1,277.8	2	1	1
2	1	1	895.8	**Delaware Water Gap, Pa.**	18327	0.1	1,293.4	4	3	2
4	3	2	867.4	Branchville, N.J.	07826	3.4	1,321.8	3	2	2
3	2	2	844.3	Unionville, N.Y.	10988	0.4	1,344.9	1	1	1
1	1	1	834.8	Glenwood, N.J.	07418	1.1	1,354.4	1	0	0
1	0	0	832.5	Vernon, N.J.	07462	2.4	1,356.7	2	1	1
2	1	1	817.5	Greenwood Lake, N.Y.	10925	2.0	1,371.7	4	3	2
4	3	2	785.6	Ft. Montgomery, N.Y.	10922	0.7	1,403.6	1	1	1
1	1	1	779.8	Peekskill, N.Y.	10566	4.8	1,409.4	3	2	1
3	2	2	755.3	Stormville, N.Y.	12582	1.7	1,433.9	1	1	1
1	1	1	748.1	Poughquag, N.Y.	12570	3.1	1,441.1	1	1	1
1	1	1	742.9	Pawling, N.Y.	12564	3.1	1,446.3	2	1	1
2	1	1	733.6	Wingdale, N.Y.	12594	3.3	1,455.6	2	1	1
2	1	1	722.1	**Kent, Conn.**	06757	0.8	1,467.1	2	1	1
2	1	1	711.0	Cornwall Bridge, Conn.	06754	0.9	1,478.2	1	1	0
1	1	0	706.2	West Cornwall, Conn.	06796	2.2	1,483.0	1	1	1
1	1	1	697.0	Falls Village, Conn.	06031	0.5	1,492.2	1	1	0
1	1	0	690.3	**Salisbury, Conn.**	06068	0.4	1,498.9	2	2	1
2	2	1	671.8	South Egremont, Mass.	01258	1.2	1,517.4	1	1	0
1	1	0	668.2	Sheffield, Mass.	01257	3.2	1,521.0	0	0	0
0	0	0	668.2	Great Barrington, Mass.	01230	1.8	1,521.0	3	2	1
3	2	1	648.8	Tyringham, Mass.	01264	0.6	1,540.4	2	1	1

POST OFFICE	ACCEPTS PACKAGES	CONVENIENCE STORE	GROCERY/ SUPERMARKET	PLACE(S) TO EAT	HOSTEL	INEXPENSIVE LODGING	DELUXE LODGING	COMMENTS
▣	•	•				🛏		
▣	•	•	🛒	🍴	🛏	🛏	🛏 $	
▣		•	🛒	🍴		🛏	🛏 $	
▣		•		🍴				
▣	•			🍴	🛏			
▣		•		🍴	🛏	🛏	🛏 $	
▣		•	🛒	🍴			🛏 $	
▣		•	🛒	🍴				
▣				🍴				
▣				🍴				
▣		•		🍴		🛏		
▣		•		🍴		🛏		
▣		•	🛒	🍴			🛏 $	
▣	•	•	🛒	🍴		🛏		
▣		•	🛒	🍴		🛏		
▣		•	🛒	🍴		🛏	🛏 $	
▣		•		🍴		🛏		
▣		•	🛒	🍴	🛏	🛏		
▣		•	🛒	🍴		🛏		
▣	•	•	🛒	🍴	🛏	🛏	🛏 $	
▣		•		🍴		🛏		
▣			🛒	🍴				
▣		•					🛏 $	
▣			🛒	🍴	🛏		🛏 $	
▣		•	🛒	🍴			🛏 $	
▣		•	🛒	🍴		🛏	🛏 $	
▣		•		🍴				
▣		•		🍴				
▣		•	🛒	🍴				
▣		•	🛒	🍴		🛏		
▣		•	🛒	🍴			🛏 $	
▣	•	•	🛒	🍴		🛏	🛏 $	
▣		•		🍴		🛏		
▣	•	•	🛒	🍴		🛏	🛏 $	
▣	•	•		🍴			🛏 $	
▣		•		🍴		🛏	🛏 $	
▣	•	•	🛒	🍴		🛏	🛏 $	
▣							🛏 $	

DAYS FROM LAST DROP AT…			TRAIL MILES FROM	DROP POINT	ZIP CODE	OFF A.T.	TRAIL MILES FROM	DAYS FROM LAST DROP AT…		
8	12	15	KATAHDIN				SPRINGER	8	12	15
MILES PER DAY								MILES PER DAY		
2	1	1	639.1	Lee, Mass.	01238	5.0	1,550.1	2	2	1
2	2	1	620.1	**Dalton, Mass.**	01226		1,569.1	1	1	1
1	1	1	611.1	**Cheshire, Mass.**	01225		1,578.1	2	1	1
2	1	1	596.6	North Adams, Mass.	01247	2.5	1,592.6	3	2	2
3	2	2	578.2	Bennington, Vt.	05201	5.0	1,611.0	6	4	3
6	4	3	538.1	**Manchester Center, Vt.**	05255	5.8	1,651.1	3	2	1
3	2	1	520.3	Danby, Vt.	05739	3.2	1,668.9	1	1	1
1	1	1	512.0	Wallingford, Vt.	05773	2.7	1,677.2	3	2	2
3	2	2	485.0	Killington, Vt.	05751	0.6	1,704.2	3	2	2
3	2	2	464.6	Woodstock, Vt.	05091	4.4	1,724.6	0	0	0
0	0	0	463.1	South Pomfret, Vt.	05067	0.9	1,726.1	1	1	1
1	1	1	452.0	West Hartford, Vt.	05084	0.3	1,737.2	1	1	1
1	1	1	443.7	Norwich, Vt.	05055	0.3	1,745.5	0	0	0
0	0	0	442.2	**Hanover, N.H.**	03755		1,747.0	5	3	3
5	3	3	408.6	Wentworth, N.H.	03282	4.3	1,780.6	1	1	1
1	1	1	398.9	Glencliff, N.H.	03238	0.4	1,790.3	2	1	1
2	1	1	389.4	**North Woodstock; Lincoln, N.H.**	03262	6.0	1,799.8	9	6	5
9	6	5	319.4	Pinkham Notch	03581		1,869.8	3	2	2
3	2	2	298.3	**Gorham, N.H.**	03581	3.6	1,890.9	6	4	3
6	4	3	256.9	**Andover, Maine**	04216	8.0	1,932.3	6	4	3
6	4	3	220.4	Rangeley, Maine	04970	9.0	1,968.8	5	3	2
5	3	2	188.2	**Stratton, Maine**	04982	5.0	2,001.0	5	3	2
5	3	2	151.2	**Caratunk, Maine**	04925	0.3	2,038.0	5	3	3
5	3	3	114.5	**Monson, Maine**	04464	4.0	2,074.7	14	10	8
14	10	8	-	Katahdin (Baxter Peak terminus)			2,189.2			

POST OFFICE	ACCEPTS PACKAGES	CONVENIENCE STORE	GROCERY/ SUPERMARKET	PLACE(S) TO EAT	HOSTEL	INEXPENSIVE LODGING	DELUXE LODGING	COMMENTS
☐	•		🛒	🍴		🛏	🛏 $	
☐		•		🍴		🛏	🛏 $	
☐		•		🍴				
☐		•	🛒	🍴		🛏	🛏 $	
☐		•	🛒	🍴		🛏	🛏 $	
☐		•	🛒	🍴	🏠	🛏	🛏 $	
☐	•	•		🍴			🛏 $	
☐		•		🍴				
☐		•				🛏	🛏 $	
☐		•	🛒	🍴		🛏	🛏 $	
☐		•						
	•							
☐		•	🛒	🍴			🛏 $	
☐		•	🛒	🍴		🛏	🛏 $	
☐			🛒					
☐					🏠			
☐	•	•	🛒	🍴	🏠	🛏	🛏 $	
	•			🍴		🛏	🛏 $	
☐	•	•	🛒	🍴	🏠	🛏	🛏 $	
☐	•	•		🍴	🏠			
☐	•		🛒	🍴	🏠	🛏	🛏 $	
☐	•	•	🛒	🍴	🏠	🛏	🛏 $	
☐		•				🛏		
☐	•	•		🍴		🛏	🛏 $	

Sample Resupply Itinerary

This is a sample itinerary; listings are not intended as recommendations for specific towns or businesses. Many towns offer multiple mail-drop options (post offices and businesses) and several places to purchase groceries. Refer to the *Appalachian Trail Thru-Hikers' Companion* and related articles on WhiteBlaze.net and other forums for more information. The *Companion* lists resupply options between major stops, particularly from New Jersey through Vermont. Be sure the businesses you choose remain in operation (even post offices can close) and still hold packages for hikers.

This chart outlines a thru-hike lasting approximately 176 days and assumes a hiker plans at least some mail drops to meet resupply needs. That said, it is possible to forgo mail drops altogether and buy food and other supplies along the way. It's also possible to arrange mail drops while you hike, although this increases the burden on the person back home who will send your packages. Be sure to factor a few "zero days" into your hike, as body and mind benefit greatly from intermittent rest. Miles here include distance to and from towns.

ETA	PICKUP/PURCHASE POINT	RESUPPLY METHOD	MILES TO NEXT STOP	DAYS TO NEXT STOP
3/23	Springer Mountain		31.7	3
3/27	Mountain Crossings at Neel Gap, Ga.	Buy	48.9	4
3/31	Hiawassee, Ga.	Buy	61.2	5
4/4	Franklin, N.C.	Buy	37.3	3
4/7	c/o Nantahala Outdoor Center 13077 Hwy. 19W Bryson City, NC 28713	Mail drop	29.6	3
4/10	c/o General Delivery Fontana Dam, NC 28733	Mail drop	110.5	9-10
4/19	c/o Bluff Mountain Outfitters 152 Bridge St. P.O. Box 114 Hot Springs, NC 28743	Mail drop	72.4	6
4/25	Erwin, Tenn.	Buy	89.9	8
5/1	c/o Kincora Hostel 1278 Dennis Cove Rd. Hampton, TN 37658	Mail drop	44.0	4
5/5	c/o Mt. Rogers Outfitters 110 Laurel Ave. (P.O. Box 546) Damascus, VA 24236	Mail drop	76.8	6
5/11	c/o Relax Inn 7253 Lee Hwy. Rural Retreat, VA 24368	Mail drop	52.4	4
5/15	Bland, Va.	Buy	49.4	4
5/19	Pearisburg, Va.	Mail drop	94.7	8

ETA	PICKUP/PURCHASE POINT	RESUPPLY METHOD	MILES TO NEXT STOP	DAYS TO NEXT STOP
5/26	Daleville, Va.	Buy	62.9	5
5/30	Glasgow, Va.	Buy	86.8	7
6/5	Waynesboro, Va.	Buy	66.5	5
6/9	Shenandoah National Park, Va. (Big Meadows Wayside)	Buy	48.9	4
6/12	Front Royal, Va.	Buy	56.7	4-5
6/16	c/o Appalachian Trail Conservancy 799 Washington St. P.O. Box 807 Harpers Ferry, WV 25425	Mail drop	45.6	4
6/19	Blue Ridge Summit, Pa.	Buy	55.6	4-5
6/22	Boiling Springs, Pa.	Buy	25.7	2
6/24	Duncannon, Pa.	Buy	70.4	5-6
6/29	c/o General Delivery Port Clinton, PA 19549	Mail drop	42.3	3-4
7/2	Palmerton, Pa.	Buy	38.4	3
7/4	c/o General Delivery Delaware Water Gap, PA 18327	Mail drop	66.1	5
7/8	Vernon, N.J.	Buy	49.9	4
7/11	Fort Montgomery, N.Y.	Buy	65.0	5
7/15	Kent, Conn.	Buy	35.0	3
7/18	Salisbury, Conn.	Buy	70.3	5-6
7/23	c/o General Delivery Dalton, MA 01226	Mail drop	26.4	2
7/25	Williamstown, Mass.	Buy	67.2	6
7/29	Manchester Center, Vt.	Buy	92.2	7
8/4	West Hartford, Vt.	Buy	10.1	1
8/5	Hanover, N.H.	Buy	74.1	6
8/11	North Woodstock, N.H.	Buy	83.4	7
8/18	Gorham, N.H.	Buy	53.0	4-5
8/22	Andover, Maine	Buy	53.5	4-5
8/26	Rangeley, Maine	Buy	46.2	3-4
8/29	Stratton, Maine	Buy	42.3	4
9/2	Caratunk, Maine	Buy	41.0	4
9/6	c/o General Delivery Monson, ME 04464	Mail drop	73.7	6
9/11	White House Landing Wilderness Camp, Maine	Buy	32.1	2-3
9/14	Abol Bridge, Maine	Buy	depends	1-2
9/15	Katahdin			

Resupply Itinerary

ETA	PICKUP/PURCHASE POINT	RESUPPLY METHOD	MILES TO NEXT STOP	DAYS TO NEXT STOP

Emergency Medical Information

Fill out the following form and keep a copy in your backpack in case you're injured on the trail. Staple a copy of this form to your itinerary and leave both forms with a trusted relative or friend.

To report a lost or injured hiker, dial 911 from the nearest phone. If necessary, authorities will contact regional search-and-rescue personnel.

PERSONAL INFORMATION

Name: ....

Trail Name: ....

Cellular telephone number: ....

E-mail address: ....

Web site URL: ....

Birthdate: ....

Blood Type: ....

Allergies: ....

Dietary Needs: ....

Preexisting Medical Conditions: ....

Medication Being Taken: ....

Drug Allergies: ....

Insurance Carrier: ....

Policy Number: ....

FAMILY PHYSICIAN

Name: ....

Address: ....

Telephone: ....

Does your physician need to be notified immediately if you are transported to a hospital?   yes   no

EMERGENCY CONTACT(S)

Name: ....

Relationship: ....

Address: ....

Telephone: ....

Name: ....

Relationship: ....

Address: ....

Telephone: ....

Name: ....

Relationship: ....

Address: ....

Telephone: ....

Leave No Trace®

Leave No Trace (www.Lnt.org) is a program designed to assist visitors with their decisions when they travel and camp on America's public lands. The program strives to educate visitors about the nature of their recreational impacts as well as techniques to prevent and minimize such impacts. It is an educational and ethical program, not a set of rules and regulations. *Guidelines specifically tailored to the A.T. can be found at <www.appalachiantrail.org/Lnt>.* The program is based on the following seven principles:

More than 3 million people use a portion of the trail each year, and, unfortunately, not all of them are aware of the Leave No Trace camping ethic. Those less knowledgeable may follow your lead—be sure to set a good example.

Plan Ahead and Prepare

You're more likely to damage natural areas if you haven't brought the right equipment or planned where you're going to stay and travel. Know local regulations. Remember: Shelters may be full, so bring a tent or tarp.

Travel and Camp on Durable Surfaces

Stay on the trail, and don't cut switchbacks. Keep off fragile trailside areas such as alpine zones. Camp in designated spots and established campsites. If you must camp elsewhere, do so out of sight of any trails and find a spot that has not been used before, being sure to leave it the way you found it. Camping in nondesignated areas that show signs of use destroys ground cover and impacts soil, increasing erosion and damaging habitat.

Dispose of Waste Properly

Pack out all trash and food waste, including that left behind by others. Do not bury trash or food, and do not burn packaging materials in campfires. Bury human and pet waste in a 6-inch-deep cathole, at least 200 feet from the nearest water source or trail. All feminine-hygiene products should be packed out. Within 100 feet of any water source, avoid using soap to wash yourself or your equipment. Use biodegradable soap and properly dispose of gray water.

Leave What You Find

Don't take flowers or other sensitive natural resources. Don't disturb historical artifacts, such as cellar holes, arrowheads, or other items.

Minimize Campfire Impacts

Know local regulations, which may prohibit campfires. Use a portable stove instead of an open fire. If you must build a fire, make a low-impact fire, use only downed wood and existing fire pits or rings, and don't add rocks to existing rings. Extinguish the fire before breaking camp. Drown out fires and empty the fire pit. Scatter leaves and twigs to cover any signs that you've been there.

Respect Wildlife

Don't feed or disturb wildlife. Store food properly to avoid attracting bears and rodents. If you bring a pet, keep it leashed.

Be Considerate of Other Visitors

Limit overnight groups to 10 or fewer persons, 25 on day trips. Minimize noise and intrusive behavior (including use of cellular phones). Share shelters and other facilities.

Worksheets are listed in **bold** type.

Index